Dedication

This book is dedicated to the job seekers and career professionals who have spent innumerable hours attempting to unravel the federal job system and commiting themselves in the face of great difficulty - to the noble task of making government work.

Reviews from Career Professionals

In my counseling sessions with students at George Mason University, I encourage students to explore a variety of career options, including federal opportunities. Kathryn's book is a well-written, accurate reference source which deals with topics ranging from learning how to network to locating federal internships. Employers continue to emphasize the importance of gaining career-related experience through experiential education. I find Kathryn's books extremely useful and frequently use them to help students navigate through the federal employment process and find opportunities.

Christine Earman Harriger, M.Ed., M.C.D.P., Career Counselor
University Career Services, George Mason University

Almost 45% of our graduate students end up working for the federal government when they finish their program here. Given the preponderance of departments, agencies, and programs within the federal government both domestically and internationally, our students find the resources available to them through our office to be of great value. When they start their studies at the Elliott School, a vast majority of them focus mainly on the Foreign Service. Although our success with placing grads in the foreign service is great, more and more of them look toward other agencies like the Department of Energy, the Department of Homeland Security, the Office of Secretary of Defense, the Department of Labor, the Defense Intelligence Agency, the Congressional Research Service, and the Government Accountability Office. Many of these agencies come to our school to talk and interview our students specifically, and we put our students in touch with contacts we have at these agencies whenever we can. One of these contacts is Kathryn Troutman's book on federal employment. The Federal Government is a huge place that can be overwhelming and frustrating for job seekers. We help our students steer their searches in the right direction, and sometimes that includes places they may never have heard of.

Paul Binkley, Associate Director Graduate Student Career Development, Elliot School of International Affairs, George Washington University

12345678910

THE STUDENT'S FEDERAL CAREER GUIDE

10 STEPS TO FIND AND WIN TOP GOVERNMENT JOBS AND INTERNSHIPS

KATHRYN KRAEMER TROUTMAN AND EMILY K. TROUTMAN

WITH CONTRIBUTIONS BY
DAVID RAIKOW, PH.D., SUSAN CUSTARD AND HARRY C. REDD III

The Resume Place

Publishers, Writers, Trainers – Federal Job Search Strategies

The Student's Federal Career Guide

Copyright 2004 by Kathryn Kraemer Troutman
ISBN 0-9647025-6-8

Published By The Resume Place, Inc.
89 Mellor Avenue, Baltimore, MD 21228
Phone: (888) 480 8265 • Fax: (410) 744-0112
Email: *resume@resume-place.com*
Website/Shopping Cart: *www.resume-place.com*
Free Student Info: *www.tenstepsforstudents.org*
Distributed by Jist, Inc., Indianapolis, IN
Available at favorite wholesalers
Printed in the United States of America by United Book Press, Baltimore, MD

See the back of this book for Resume Place titles and information, including Ten Steps for Students™ PowerPoint Curriculum for Career Professionals and Instructors. Institutional license is available for CD-ROM student resume samples and templates. Quantity discounts are available for books.

We have been careful to provide accurate information throughout this book, but it is possible that errors and omissions have been introduced. Website addresses and Federal job information may be updated and revised at any time. The resume samples in the book and on the CD-ROM are of real recent graduates who have given permission to use their resumes in this book. Their names, social security numbers, and other specific job information have been changed.

Book Credits

Interior Layout Designer
Cover Design
CD-ROM Interface Design
MJR Media www.mjrmedia.com

Development Editors
Sarah Blazucki
Bonny Kraemer Day

**Federal Human Resources
Consultant and Editor**
Harry C. Redd III

**University Career Counselor,
Technical Advisor**
Kelli Poehls
North Dakota State University

Proofreader
Bonita Kraemer

Resume Designs / CD-ROM
Carla Waskiewicz
Jessica Coffey
Mark Reichenbacher
Sarah Blazucki
Bonny Kraemer Day
Stacie Berg

Glossary
David Raikow, Ph.D.
Harry C. Redd III

Index
L. Pilar Wyman
Wyman Indexing
www.wymanindexing.com

Editorial Assistants
Katie Rathbun
Lisa Shaw

Other Books by Kathryn K. Troutman

Ten Steps to a Federal Job & CD-ROM
Ten Steps to a Federal Job – Trainer's Guide
Federal Resume Guidebook & CD-Rom, 1st, 2nd, 3rd Ed., Jist, Publisher
Creating Your High School Resume, 1st and 2nd Ed., Jist, Publisher

J. Brian Atwood served for six years as administrator of the U.S. Agency for International Development during the administration of President William Clinton.

In the Clinton administration, Atwood led the transition team at the State Department and was Under Secretary of State for Management prior to his appointment as head of USAID. In December 1998, President Clinton nominated Atwood as Ambassador to Brazil. He withdrew prior to Senate confirmation to create Citizens International, an organization that designs and manages public and private social development investments to meet the needs of developing nations.

Atwood was an adjunct lecturer at Harvard's JFK School from 1999 to 2001 and was the Sol M. Linowitz Professor for International Affairs at Hamilton College in 2001.

Atwood's career in foreign policy dates back to 1966 when he joined the Foreign Service and served in the American Embassies in Cote d'Ivoire and Spain. He served as legislative adviser for foreign and defense policy to Senator Thomas F. Eagleton (D-Mo.) from 1972-1977. During the Carter Administration he served as Assistant Secretary of State for Congressional Relations. He was Dean of Professional Studies and Academic Affairs at the Foreign Service Institute in 1981-82.

Atwood was the first president of the National Democratic Institute for International Affairs (NDI) from 1986-1993 and built this democratic development institution into a major international force for the promotion of democracy. He received an honorary doctorate from American University in 1995 for his work in promoting human rights and democratic values. He has received numerous other awards for public service, including the Secretary of State's Distinguished Service Award.

Foreword

Our political process has generated controversy about the role of the federal government, some legitimate, some ideological. Yet, few politicians would suggest that the efficient management of taxpayers' resources to preserve our security, protect our food supply, maintain our health or provide for our general welfare are at issue. In fact, the threats to our wellbeing as a nation make service in the federal government more important than ever.

The Hubert H. Humphrey Institute of Public Affairs and some 281 other public affairs colleges prepare young Americans for careers in public service. The fields they select are as varied as the challenges our nation faces: international relations, public health, environmental protection, social services, community development, urban planning, education policy, etc. In all of these areas, the federal government is taking the lead working with state and local governments to provide for the welfare of the American people.

How does one discover the career opportunities that abound within the government? Every agency has different application procedures. Most operate under the guidance of the Office of Personnel Management, but national security considerations create exceptions for departments like State, Defense, Homeland Security and the Intelligence Community. This book unlocks the secrets of the application process and provides invaluable advice to those who wish to serve the public at the federal level. Kathryn and Emily Troutman have performed a wonderful service by making this book available.

After 24 years of experience at the federal level, I can personally attest to the satisfaction one derives from a career in government. I started near the bottom and ended as a Presidential appointee. In some ways, finding the political jobs was easier than penetrating the bureaucratic red tape in applying for the career service in the lower ranks. I only regret this book was not available when I began my career some 30 years ago. Its readers will be assisted in finding the public service career they want. I hope they will also find the satisfaction I derived from public service.

J. Brian Atwood
Dean, Humphrey Institute of Public Affairs
University of Minnesota

Acknowledgements

David Raikow, Ph.D. and **Susan Custard** drafted the first editions of the steps to get the information organized and presented. Thank you for your contributions and structure for this book. A huge amount of research and thought went into all the drafts!

Harry C. Redd III, Senior Human Resources Policy Analyst from the Merit Systems Protection Board. He retired from MSPB on a Friday and started on the Student's Federal Career Guide on Monday. Thank you, Harry, for your technical knowledge and writing skill!

Student Case Study Volunteers – Thank you all for sharing your success stories, resumes, KSAs and announcements. The book and CD would not be as interesting without your success stories and strategies! Thank you to Scott Holland, Lisa Reichenbacher, Jen Grine, Brian Roberts, Sheri A. Bodolosky-Bettis, Kalvis Kraemer, Ligita Kraemer, Pierre Viens, Nicole Santana, Erickson Young, Annie Yager, Ardrianna French, Meredith Jones and Kelli Roscoe.

We appreciate the **University Career Counselor** support and comments of book reviewers which included Kelli Poehls, Career Specialist, North Dakota State University (who tirelessly read the entire book and gave comments for students throughout); Christine Earman Harriger, M.Ed., M.C.D.P., Roberta Kaskel, Career Counselor, University of Maryland, College Park; Jeanine Dick, Employer Relations Coordinator, Graduate Career Center, George Washington University; and Paul Binkley, Associate Director, Graduate Student Career Development, Elliott School of International Affairs, The George Washington University.

Thanks to the **Federal Human Resource** experts who contributed to this book: Ligaya Fernandez, Harry C. Redd III, and professional policy staff at the Merit Systems Protection Board; Mariana Pardo, USAJOBS Team Leader, Office of Personnel Management; John Shaw, HR Director, GSA Great Lakes Region; Rachel C. Friedland, Assistant Marketing Communications Consultant, and Diane Castiglione, Director of Recruitment, State Department; A. Mae Hazelton, Army Material Command, Engineering Directorate; James J. Wilson, Former Director, Presidential Management Fellowship; Sheila Reid Dent, Chief,

Employment and Compensation Management Division, and Edmond G. Gauvreau, AIA, U.S. Army Corps of Engineers; Beth Ann Ritter, Government Accountability Office; Brian Friel, Editor, National Journal; John M. Palguta, Vice President for Policy and Research, and Carolyn Chang, Program Manager, Partnership for Public Service.

We are appreciative to Jist, Inc. and especially Tom Doherty and Bob Grilliot for distributing the book to libraries, schools, bookjobbers and Internet booksellers!

We would finally like to thank our family and Resume Place staff for tolerating another federal resume writing book and CD! We'd especially like to thank the Resume Place Federal Resume Writing Team: Sarah Blazucki, Stacie Berg, Jessica Coffey, Jacqueline Allen and Carla Waskiewicz for their edits and case study reviews. We particularly want to thank Bonny Kraemer Day, Kathryn's sister, and who was the Office Manager for Resume Place for 20 years, who came back for the summer from her music teacher's job to edit another federal resume book.

Kathryn Kraemer Troutman, Author, Publisher and President, The Resume Place, Inc. and Emily K. Troutman, Author and Candidate for a Master's in Public Policy, University of Minnesota.

1 2 3 4 5 6 7 8 9 10

TABLE OF CONTENTS

10 Steps to Find and Win Top Government Jobs and Internships

CD-ROM Case Studies

Federal Resume and KSA Templates and Samples in Microsoft Word and PDF format

Susan Anthony, B.A., Political Science, USAID New Entry Professional

Marie Revellier, B.S., Biology, Biologist, Federal Career Intern, NIH

Ravi Nair, M.S., Computer Science, Special Agent, Information Assurance, FBI

Erickson Young, B.A., Government and Spanish, Peace Corps Volunteer

Andrea Fritchie, B.A., Human Ecology, Visitor Information Assistant, GS-5, USDA, USFS

Calvin Kline, A.A., Aviation Maintenance Technology, Aircraft Mechanic, WG-8852-5, DOD

Nicole Santiago, B.A., Communications, Management Analyst, GS-343-9, CMS

Meredith L. Jones, Junior, B.S., Civil Engineering, Student Trainee, BOR

Scott Hampstead, B.S., Mechanical Engineering, Career Mngmt Internship, GS-0830-7, USACE

David F. Raikow, Ph.D., Biology, Research Aquatic Biologist, GS-0401-11, NOAA

Lauren T. Dobbin, Ph.D., Chemistry, Chemist, Forensic Scientist, FBI

Laura E. Richardson, B.A., Graphic Design, Administrative Assistant, GS-0318-4/5, USDA, FSIS

Kelly A. Rodgers, M.B.A., Finance, Accountant, Navy

Jennifer Wilson, M.A., Criminology, Inspector General, GS-0343-09, DHS

Simone Ledeen, M.B.A., Finance, International Finance, Government Contractor - Baghdad

Introduction

Why go Federal?
If you're reading this book, you are probably aware that the private industry job market is a jungle. This is especially true for recent graduates—today, college graduates are more likely than high school dropouts to be unemployed. Having a college degree no longer ensures that you will have the job of your dreams after graduation. In fact, in today's competitive job market you may find yourself in competition with those who have multiple advanced degrees or 5 to 10 years of job experience!

Your choice to pursue a job in government is a smart move. The United States federal government is the largest employer in the U.S. The government employs 2.6 million people in jobs that range from biology to art restoration to law enforcement. In addition, the average federal employee is over 46 years of age, and two of every five are eligible now to retire. Agencies are scrambling to find a new, younger workforce…YOU!

Work in the federal government is often more financially rewarding than work in private industry. The average entry level starting salary in government is $26,000 to $37,000 per year. The government may also offer full benefits including; comprehensive health insurance, 401K with matching funds, 10 paid holidays annually, plus 13 days paid vacation to start! Agencies also have the discretion to pay you a signing bonus or pay your student loan debt. In addition, the federal government often offers more workplace flexibility than corporate America. All of these factors add up to a great opportunity for a successful and rewarding career opportunity for you.

The Federal Hiring Process
The federal job application process is complex. Government job announcements are not found in traditional places like newspapers or on internet job sites like Monster.com. You will have to dig deeper and look harder to find job announcements specific to your skills and experience. You will need to address each specific job application with a federal resume and supporting documents.

After you read this book you will know how to:

- Find job openings and vacancy announcements
- Interpret job titles
- Write a federal resume and supporting documents
- Apply for a federal job
- Get hired in the right job for you!

The Student's Federal Career Guide is the **only book** with comprehensive information written just for recent college graduates. It is an essential resource as you maneuver through the federal application process for the first time.
In this book you will find:

- Ten Steps—painstakingly jargon-free
- Interactive multimedia CD-ROM including:
    - 10 successful student case studies
    - Sample federal resumes
    - Sample federal application components including KSAs and cover letters
    - Hotlinks to on-line job search databases, resume writing resources and MORE
- Glossary—to interpret complex instructions and confusing federal terms
- Information and resources on opportunities available only to you, the recent graduate, including insider tips on:
    - Federal Career Management Internship
    - Presidential Management Fellows
    - Student Career Internship Program (SCEP)
    - Student Temporary Employment Program (STEP)
    - Outstanding Scholars
- Index—for quick reference

The best way to use this book is simply follow the steps straight through. But if you're up against a deadline, skip right to Step 6 for great instructions on preparing your federal resume!

The text includes important information about federal internships not collected in any other publication. You will learn how to find internships and successfully compete for these positions.

Susan Anthony
B.A. Communications
U.S. Agency for International Development

This picture is of me eating a traditional Indian meal with my friends. In high school, my church raised $250,000 for developing countries. I got to represent the kids at my church on a trip to India. Ever since then, I knew I wanted to do something to contribute.

I found out about the U.S. Agency for International Development (USAID) through the person who organized my church's trip to India. The job was listed on usajobs.opm.gov. Even though travel isn't a part of my job, I still feel connected to what's happening in other countries. It feels good to know I am part of such an awesome organization.

Read Susan's federal resume on the CD-ROM.

1 2 3 4 5 6 7 8 9 10

Why network?

For many students, finding a summer job or internship means canvassing door-to-door or contacting many managers of businesses or organizations to gain information about jobs and internships. Networking is just a sophisticated form of the door-to-door research. This step is more important than you may realize. The federal government is huge and the hiring process is both complex and decentralized. Visualize the federal government as an iceberg (generally huge and imposing!), which you can see only a small part of at one time.

Networking will help in several ways as you nagivate the federal hiring process. You may 1) become familiar with the hiring process; 2) gain information about current and upcoming jobs; and 3) learn about specific agency missions and cultures.

1. Become familiar with the hiring process

When you talk to people who work in government, you will soon realize that each individual has taken a different path to get that particular job. While this may look confusing at first, this is also true of private industry. For example, applying for a job at Microsoft would require a different hiring process than applying for a job at Dell.

Hiring practices reflect distinctive corporate needs and cultures. Agencies and departments use specific vocabulary and sometimes require unique online applications systems. You can learn a lot about what to expect by talking to people on the inside.

2. Gain information about current and upcoming jobs

To begin your search for federal job listings or announcements, you can go to *www.usajobs.opm.gov*. However, *www.usajobs.opm.gov* does not list most federal internship programs, and finding the right announcement for you can be challenging. If you build a network, or support system if you will, you may hear about jobs before they are posted and know where to look for them. You will also learn about how jobs are described on usajobs. One of the most common job titles in the federal government is Program Analyst. The terms used to describe duties of a Program Analyst may include "help agency fulfill its mission" and "conduct programmatic research." But what do those terms mean? The meanings vary by agency. Your government network can help you interpret job announcements and determine if a job is right for you before you spend a lot of time applying.

3. Learn about specific agency missions and cultures

Students and recent graduates often make the mistake of conducting a very narrow job search. For example, students of international relations often think that the State Department is the only place for people with this type of experience. People who are already in government positions can give you great tips on how to expand your job search.

They may work with a little-known agency that would be perfect for you. For instance, have you ever heard of the National Geospatial-Intelligence Agency or the Southern European Task Force? Agency names also change from time to time and new departments, like the Department of Homeland Security, are especially challenging to navigate.

How to Network

Due to security concerns, it is virtually impossible to walk off the street and into a federal building. Therefore, you must find alternate ways to connect with people on the inside. Compared to local and state governments, the federal government has relatively few street-level employees.

The most visible federal government employees are often the least accessible, such as those featured on television's *West Wing*. The people in such jobs are also politically appointed, not hired. Political appointees make up only 0.001% of all federal jobs! As a recent graduate, you probably want to set your sights on more behind-the-scenes positions. Here are some basic strategies to make the task less daunting:

Start with people you know. Don't be embarrassed to cash in favors from family and friends. Now is the time to call up your long lost Uncle Fritz and let him know you are in the market for a federal job.

Do your research. Federal employees and managers are often more than happy to speak with students about their jobs. But you will get more insightful advice from people if you know a little about what they do and how they fit into the system. Take time to look at organizational charts and agency missions. These can be found online.

Don't expect a miracle. He may be your uncle or your best friend from college, but unlike some private industry companies, individuals truly cannot do anything to advance or influence your application. Try to remember that a network is an opportunity to learn, but in the end the federal government cares about what you know, not who you know.

Master the informational interview. Informational interviews are a great, non-threatening way to approach people. Simply call or e-mail the person and ask for 20 minutes of their time to inquire about their job and career. If you express a genuine interest in your interviewer, you let them know that you are not simply looking to make "connections" or get a job. Stick to the time limit you mentioned, and be sure to send a thank-you note and periodic updates on your search.

Where to Network

Your Career Services Office
The career services office of your school can provide you with many different services. Many career services offices now manage comprehensive placement websites – a good place to start when looking for a job opportunity. Additionally, they typically offer the following services to assist you:

- Resume development/feedback
- Career workshops
- Interview coaching
- Assessment tools
- Job search tools/strategies
- Dress-for-success tips
- Orientation to their services
- One-on-one career counseling
- Employer information

• Benefits information and assessment
• Career days/fairs
• Mentoring
• Externships

The majority of these services are offered at no cost to students or alumni. Career services offices are especially useful at large schools or schools with an established government relationship. But even at small schools, the career services office often coordinates formal internship programs like the Presidential Management Fellows Program (PMFP, formerly PMI Program), the Emerging Leaders program (a career internship program at the Department of Health and Human Services), and other internship and development opportunities. See Step 2 for more information on internships.

Your Academic Program
Federal employers often develop relationships directly with college professors or departments (School of Business, Engineering, etc.). These relationships are encouraged by the college or university and offer opportunities to enhance placement for the best and the brightest—since the candidates are clearly visible to professors and instructors. Many employers will work with the individual college to provide career information, student briefings, and provide coaches and mentors.

Identify your professors' connection with the school's career program. Introduce yourself and become known to your professors. Though it's sometimes hard to believe, they went to college once too. They have access to another valuable network of friends and colleagues who may be able to help you. Don't be afraid to ask, "Can you recommend a friend or co-worker who could help me navigate the federal system or tell me about their career in government?"

Alumni and Alumni Associations
Every college or university has an alumni association. Most colleges rely heavily on alumni groups to act as coaches and mentors, provide fund-raising for scholarships, and offer job opportunities to current students. College alumni may have a better understanding of your curriculum and can give you insightful, directed career advice. The easiest way to find alumni groups is the career services office or your college or university's website.

Professional Associations

There are hundreds of professional associations and groups in the United States, representing every single occupation and particular facets of an occupation. Internet searches are a good way to start, though for a comprehensive list of associations in your field, you should consult your school or local reference librarian. Libraries usually own one or more directories of professional associations, which list every possible group and give information about how to join.

Most associations offer low-cost student memberships with great benefits like workshops, newsletters, job bulletin boards, and member lists. Member phone and e-mail lists can be a great way to make contact with people and conduct informational interviews.

Conclusion

It may seem time consuming, but networking works! Many federal employees found out about their jobs by staying connected. Just remember, unless you are a political appointee, do not expect your connections alone to help you land a job. Former President Theodore Roosevelt created the original structure of the federal hiring process so that it would be fair and impartial. So join professional organizations, send polite e-mails, but leave the fruit baskets and crisp $100 bills at home.

Top Questions to Ask in an Informational Interview

• How did you find your position?

• What education or experience is necessary for a job like yours?

• What kind of a job would people in your position look for next?

• How do you spend an average day at work?

• What skills or attributes do you consider crucial to your job?

• What aspects of your job do you love/hate?

• What other agencies do you work with?

• Which professional associations would someone in your field belong to?

• Can you recommend someone else that I might interview?

Q&A with John Shaw, General Services Administration, Student Human Resources Recruiter

Q: Can you briefly explain what your agency does and your role there?

A: GSA helps federal agencies better serve the public by offering, at best value, superior workplaces, expert solutions, acquisition services, and management policies. Simply put, GSA is the business arm of the Federal Government. We help other Agencies accomplish their missions by providing office space, supplies, telecommunications, IT, and vehicle support. For further information our website is *www.gsa.gov.* I serve as the Regional Employment Officer for the Great Lakes Region and as the GSA National College Recruitment Coordinator.

Q: Where can students and new grads find information about your internship programs?

A: Students should contact the Human Resources office in the geographic area where they wish to work. We have 11 regional offices.

Q: Which students/new grads do you target? Is there a particular profile?

A: For a few of our jobs we require specific degrees, such as engineering, architecture, information technology, industrial technology, and automotive technology, but for many of our jobs, most majors are acceptable. However, we like to see students who have some coursework in business, economics, management, etc. We are looking for students and new grads who have a sincere interest in public service and are enthusiastic, motivated, and able to work as part of a team.

Q: How long does it take to get your application reviewed, and how can young people best prepare to be competitive?

A: It depends on the agency, the appointment authority, the number of positions being filled, etc. With GSA it may typically take from four to six weeks. Most government agencies afford applicants the opportunity to complete an online resume either through the Office of Personnel Management's USAJOBS website or on their own automated systems. My recommendation is that applicants should look at their current resume, see how closely it conforms to what the agency is asking for, and make the necessary changes before applying for a specific job. Recent grads should be prepared to submit copies of their transcripts.

Q: What are the top three most common mistakes that recent grads or students make in their applications or during interviews?

A:
1. Incorrect spelling and poor grammar [in their applications].
2. Not becoming informed about the employer prior to the interview. This is inexcusable with all the information available on the web.
3. Not following up with the agency after an interview.

Q: If you could give a student or new grad two strong tips for how to successfully enter the federal government, what would they be?

A: Probe to find out what hiring authorities a particular Agency uses, that is, Student Career Employment Program (SCEP), Federal Career Intern Program (FCIP), Presidential Fellows, etc., because Federal agencies have different preferences for hiring. Then find out the qualification requirements for those programs and, assuming that you meet the requirements, make a contact via e-mail, phone, or letter or all three indicating your interest in their positions and your eligibility for those programs.

FIND YOUR AGENCY

Marie Revellier
B.S. Biology
Department of Natural Resources

I wanted to work with animals from the time I was nine years old. I'm from a farm town and was constantly taking in sick or injured animals. It drove my parents crazy! The first animal I took in was a baby squirrel. I loved everything about it—trying to figure out what a baby squirrel eats, finding a warm place for it and even waking up at 2 a.m. to feed it.

After college, I considered veterinary school but wanted to work for a while first. I volunteered at a vet's office throughout college and used that job to help me get into the Department of Natural Resources. It is the perfect department for me. I actually get paid to take care of stray animals.

Read Marie's federal resume on the CD-ROM.

What agency and job title will be right for you?

To select an agency of interest to you, there are three steps to follow:
1) create the "mission statement match"; 2) consider location; and,
3) examine opportunities.

Mission Statement Match

Your choice to pursue a career in public service gives you the opportunity to choose an agency whose mission matches yours. This is a great privilege and one of the many underrated and unrecognized benefits of working for the federal government.

A mission statement is an organization's vision of its purpose and work philosophy. Mission statements are often a practical guide and contain valuable information about each agency's goals, structure, and culture.

You can use your network to gain a better understanding of agencies' missions, services, and customers. To find mission statements, visit the homepage of any federal agency. Links to many federal agencies can be found on the CD-ROM which accompanies this book.

Location, Location, Location

So you really want to work for the White House, but you don't want to leave Wyoming? Unfortunately, you may need to change your plans. On the other hand, Wyoming may offer plenty of opportunities with the National Park Service and Bureau of Land Management, among others.

Contrary to popular belief, most federal jobs are NOT located only in Washington, D.C. In fact, Denver, Colorado ranks second among cities with federal employees. As a federal employee, you may find yourself eating lunch while overlooking the beach on a Hawaiian Island (working as a civilian for the U.S. Navy or for Defense Finance & Accounting Service), or watching buffalo graze in Wyoming (working for Bureau of Land Management or Department of Interior). Find out which agencies are based in your city before you begin.

Job Availability

For job seeking purposes, you can divide federal agencies into two categories—*classic* and *hot*. You can count on certain classic agencies to continually hire people with your skill set. For example, if your degree is in biology, the Department of Agriculture and the National Park Service would be natural places to consider. If your degree was in business, you might find jobs in an agency which specializes in business services, such as General Services Administration, Small Business Administration, and Department of Commerce. But remember, every federal agency has at least some employees who provide basic business services!

Some federal agencies simply hire more employees than others based on how much money is available and our nation's current employment focus. These agencies are considered *hot*. As this book is written, the Department of Homeland Security (DHS) is definitely *hot*. As a result of current national events, the new department was created and is now experiencing significant hiring increases. Within that department, many new jobs were created particularly in Customs and Border Patrol and other DHS agencies. Also *hot* agencies would be any Department of Defense agency or military base. Again, because of the ongoing wartime activities, the warfighters need extensive support from civilians in the U.S. and abroad to complete their peace missions. To find federal jobs, it helps to stay abreast of the news and take notice when Congress appropriates money for particular agencies.

Some federal jobs are not placed within the large federal agencies. Some of these jobs can be found on Capitol Hill in Congress. To find a job with a legislator, you should go straight to your state Senator's or Representative's website, or phone his/her office directly. The Senate and House have their own hiring rules and processes. Many agencies, especially in Washington, D.C., hire employees whose jobs include communicating with Congress. Such jobs represent opportunities if your interests lie in that direction. Remember to find organizational charts and obtain more details through informational interviews. (See Step 1)

Find Your Federal Job Chart

The *Find Your Federal Job* chart, translates your major into selected federal job titles. Sometimes it is difficult to find jobs simply because you are not familiar with government language. Federal job titles are not the same as those in private industry. The chart makes Step 2 easier for you.

For example, if you are a Liberal Arts major and your skills are writing, analysis, and research, your target federal jobs may be Program and Management Analyst, Writer-Editor, Public Affairs Specialist, or Management Assistant. In private industry, your target job titles may be Communications Specialist, Public Relations Specialist, Administrative Assistant, or Program Assistant. This chart gives examples of job titles that can apply to multiple academic backgrounds.

To use the *Find Your Federal Job* chart, simply locate your major and match it with the job titles and agencies. It is impossible to list every agency that hires people with your degree. The chart on the CD-ROM also includes both *classic* agencies, which would historically hire people with your degree, and *hot* agencies, which have a current need for people with your skills. If you cannot find your specific degree, try to find a similar one. You can also research similar degrees to get more ideas. For instance, if you majored in Biology and focused in Botany, look at the opportunities for all biology majors to see what else may be available.

Notes To the Chart

The Beauty of Many Federal Career Opportunities

For those among you who are yet undecided as to your specific career path, it often doesn't matter what your degree is in to obtain federal employment. For many occupations, education is a substitute for qualifying experience at the entry level grades. Possessing a Bachelor's degree is enough to qualify you for many jobs.

This doesn't mean that all degrees will be treated as equal when applicants are assessed. Some degrees are better than others at preparing you for a particular occupation, and some jobs absolutely require specific education.

However, solid grades in fields as diverse as psychology, English, and history (and other liberal arts fields) can make you highly competitive for many fields. If you haven't already decided on a career field, consider one such as human resources specialist, administrative officer, management analyst, public information specialist, program analyst, immigration inspector, housing management, and general and criminal investigator.

Program Analysts and Management Analysts

These are popular job titles in federal agencies. What do these jobs entail? Employees in these titles conduct analyses and advise management on the effectiveness of government programs and operations, or on the productivity and efficiency of agency management, or both. These jobs require knowledge of the substantive nature of agency programs and activities, knowledge of agency missions, policies and objectives, management principles and processes, and analytical and evaluative techniques and methods. These jobs require skill in applying fact-finding and investigative techniques, oral and written communications, and development of presentations and reports. They do not require specialized subject-matter expertise in a specialized line of work.

Some Elusive Job Titles

Some job titles that seem familiar and carry a promise of exciting careers include "Special Agent" and "Researcher," especially when the latter is used in medical or scientific settings such as the National Institutes of Health or the Center for Disease Control. But when we search for these titles, we don't find them. Why?

Typically, these are "working titles" rather than official titles. As a result, they may not be used in vacancy announcements. So exercise your analytical and investigative skills and think "investigator" for special agent, especially criminal investigator (the government also has general investigators). For jobs in agencies such as NIH and CDC, think in terms of the kind of work they do. Look for titles like Research Microbiologist. Recognize, however, that many of these jobs are senior level, and senior medical researchers have an MD in addition to doctorates in specialized scientific areas.

MAJOR	TARGET JOB TITLES
Accounting	Accounting Specialist, Budget Analyst, Contract Specialist, Auditor, Cost Accountant, Financial Analyst
Aerospace Engineering	Aerospace Engineering, Safety Engineer, Materials Engineer
Agricultural Engineering	Agricultural Engineer, Range Technician, Safeguarding, Intervention, and Trade Compliance Officer
American Studies	Researcher, Writer-Editor, Policy Analyst, Program & Mgt. Analyst
Ancient and Medieval Art and Archaeology	Cryptanalyst, Intelligence Analyst, Clandestine Service
Ancient Near Eastern Studies	Cryptanalyst, Intelligence Analyst, Special Agent, Clandestine Service
Animal Sciences	Wildlife Biologist, Animal Scientist
Arabic	Foreign Languages, Cryptanalyst, Intelligence Analyst, Special Agent, Toponymist
Art History	Cryptanalyst, Special Agent, Intelligence Analyst, Archives Specialist
Asian Languages and Literatures	Foreign Language Studies, Cryptanalyst, Special Agent, Passport Officer
Biology	Biological Science Group, Forensic Chemist, Imagery Intelligence Analyst, Fishery Biologist
Biomedical Engineering	Biomedical Engineering, Research Ecologist Rhizosphere
Botany	Safeguarding, Intervention & Trade Compliance officer, Plant Protection and Quarantine Officer, Assistant Manager, Plant Materials Center (NRCS)
Biosystems & Agricultural Engineering	
Business Administration	Contract Specialist, Acquisitions, Business & Industry Series, Supply Analyst, Grants and Agreements Speciaist (Forest Service), Realty Specialist, Restructuring Analyst, Inventory Management Specialist, Industrial Security Specialist
Cell and Development Biology	NIH Research
Chemical Engineering and Materials Science	Chemical Engineering and Materials Science
Chemistry	Chemist, Physical Scientist, Forensic Chemist, Imagery Intelligence Analyst
Civil Engineering	Civil Engineer, Construction Representative
Classical and Near Eastern Studies	Cryptanalyst, Special Agent, Intelligence Analyst, Clandestine Service
Clinical Laboratory Science	NIH Clinical Research Positions
Communication Studies	Writer-Editor, Public Affairs Specialist, Program & Management Analyst

MAJOR	TARGET JOB TITLES
Computer Engineering	Info Tech Spec, Project Mgr, Prog. Mgr; Comp Scientist; Telecom. Spec.
Computer Science & Information Sciences	Quality Assurance Specialist, Patent Examiner (Electrical & Computer Engineering, Computer Science)
Conservation Biology	Biologist, Ecologist, Wildlife Refuge Manager, Environmental Prot. Spec.
Construction Management	Facilities Management Spec., Realty Specialist
Creative Writing	Writer-Editor, Public Affairs Specialist, Program & Management Analyst, Speechwriter
Criminal Justice	Physical Security Specialist, Intelligence Operations Specialist, Security Specialist, Investigator
Crop, Soil, and Pest Management	Agronomist, Agriculture Extension, Entomologist, Soil Conservation, Soil Scientist
Cultural Studies	Cryptanalyst, Special Agent, Intelligence Analyst, Clandestine Service, Foreign Service Officer
East Asian Studies	Cryptanalyst, Special Agent, Intelligence Analyst, Clandestine Service
Ecology	Ecologist, Biologist, Fisheries Biologist, Wildlife Biologist, Physical Scientist
Economics	Economist, Statistician, Mathemetician, Imagery Intelligence Analyst, Economic Research Analyst
Education	Teacher, Training Specialist, Geospatial Intelligence Instructor, Education Specialist, Transformation Facilitator
Educational Policy and Administration	Policy Analyst, Program and Management Analyst, Legislative Analyst
Emergency Health Services	Emergency Preparedness, Emergency Services Dispatcher (OA), Paramedic
Emergency Medical Technician	Firefighter, Emergency Medical Technician, Law Enforcement Communications Assistant, Disaster Recovery & Operations Specialist, Range Technician (Initial Attack Fire/aviation Dispatcher), Occupational Safety & Health
English	Writer-Editor, Public Affairs Specialist, Program & Management Analyst, Legislative Analyst
English as a Second Language	ESOL Teacher, International Relations, Education Specialist
Environmental Science	Biologist, Ecologist, Wildlife Refuge Manager, Environmental Prot. Spec., Program Manager
Epidemiology	Epidemiologist
Finance	Financial Analyst, Financial Management Specialist, Auditor, Financial & Program Analyst

MAJOR	TARGET JOB TITLES
Fisheries and Wildlife	Fisheries Biologist, Wildlife Biologist, Biologist, Ecologist
Food Science	Researcher, Interdisciplinary: Research Food Technologist/Chemist/Physical Scientist, Dietitian (Lipid/Cardiovascular Disease Specialist), Public Health Nutritionist, Consumer Safety Officer, Agricultural Program Specialist, Public Health Nutritionist-Dietitian
Forestry	Forester, Forestry Technician, Wildland Fire Program Manager
Geographic Information Science	GIS specialist - linked with scientific field (Biology, Geology), Regional ISMS/GeoBOB Data Steward (interdisciplinary)
Global Studies	Environmental Protection Specialist, International Relations Specialist, Import Policy Analyst, Intelligence Analyst, Intelligence Operations Specialist
Graphic Design	Graphics Design, Visual Information Specialist, Multimedia Designer
Health Journalism	Writer-Editor, Public Affairs Specialist, Health Insurance Specialist
Health Services Research, Policy, and Administration.	Health Insurance Specialist, Health Information Specialist, Public Health Advisor, Public Health Analyst, Social Insurance Specialist (Claims Representative), Medical Records Administration Specialist
Hispanic Studies	Foreign Languages, International Broadcaster (Spanish)
History	Signals Analysis, Cryptanalyst, Intelligence Analyst, Program Analyst, Researcher, Archives Specialist
Human Resource Development	Human Resources, Equal Employment Opportunity Specialist, Management Specialist, Labor-Management Specialist
Industrial Engineering	Industrial Specialist, Occupational Safety and Health Specialist
Information Networking	Information Technology Specialist, Project Manager
Information Technology Infrastructure	Information Technology Specialist, Systems Analyst
International Business	Business Protocol Officer, Risk Analyst/Forecaster, Strategic Consultant, International Relations Specialist, International Economist, International Cooperative Program Specialist, Export Policy Analyst
International Relations	Center Adjudications Officer, Import Policy Analyst, International Activities Assistant, Research Analyst, Program Officer, Desk Officer, Regional Security Officer, Special Agent, Systems Analyst, Mediator

MAJOR	TARGET JOB TITLES
Japanese	Foreign Languages, Cryptanalyst, Intelligence Specialist, Passport Officer
Journalism	Writer-Editor, Public Affairs Specialist, Program & Management Analyst
Latin	Foreign Languages, Intelligence Operations Specialist
Law	Attorney-Advisor, Staff Attorney, Paralegal Specialist, Administrative Investigator, Policy Analyst
Legal Studies	Paralegal Specialist, Management Specialist
Liberal Studies	Community Outreach Specialist, Intelligence Operations Specialist, Industrial Security Specialist
Library Science	Librarian, Archivist, Media Specialist, Archives Specialist
Linguistics	Signals Analysis, Cryptanalyst, Intelligence Analyst
Management Information Systems	Information Technology Specialist
Management of Technology	Information Technology Specialist, Program Analyst
Manufacturing Technology	Quality Assurance Specialist, Production Management, Industrial Security Specialist
Marketing	Contract Specialist, Purchasing Agent, Business & Industry Specialist, Consumer Affairs Specialist
Marketing and Logistics Management	Logistics Management Specialist, General Supply Specialist, Transportation Specialist
Mass Communication	Writer-Editor; Public Information Specialist; Audio-Visual Specialist
Materials Science and Engineering	Materials Management Specialist, Fire Management Officer
Mathematics	Signals Analysis, Cryptanalyst, Intelligence Analyst, Quality Assurance Specialist, Statistician, Mathemetician
Mechanical Engineering	Mechanical Engineer
Microbiology, Immunology, and Cancer Biology	Microbiologist, Biologist
Molecular Biology	Molecular Biology, Health Scientist
Molecular, Cellular, Devel. Biology and Genetics	Geneticist
Multimedia	Multimedia specialist, Visual Information Specialist, Audio-Visual Specialist
Natural Resources and Environmental Studies	Natural Conservation Resource Specialist, Environ. Protection Specialist
Network Administration	Information Technology Specialist, Systems Analyst
Nursing	Nurse, Health Insurance Specialist, Psychiatric Nurse, Surgical Technician

MAJOR	TARGET JOB TITLES
Operations and Management Science	Production Manager, Program Manager, Disaster Recovery & Oper. Spec.
Pharmaceutics	Researcher, Pharmacist
Philosophy	Intelligence Operations Specialist, Ethics Program Specialist
Physical Education and Recreation	Morale, Recreation & Welfare Counselor, Fitness Instruction, Recreation Planner
Physics	Physics, Health Physicist, Occupational Safety and Health Specialist
Planning—See Urban and Regional Planning	Realty Specialist, Housing Management Specialist
Plant Biology	Botanist, Plant Pathologist, Plant Physiologist
Political Science	Policy Analyst, Congressional Affairs Specialist, Legislative Analyst, Transformation Facilitator
Psychology	Victim Specialist, Grant Program Specialist, Transformation Facilitator
Public Affairs	Public Affairs Specialist, Community Outreach Specialist
Public Health Administration	Health Systems Specialist, Health Information Specialist
Public Policy	Public Policy Analyst, International Trade Compliance Analyst, International Relations Specialist, Speech Writer, Foreign Service Officer
Rehabilitation Science	Rehabilitation Specialist, Fitness Specialist
Retail Merchandising	Supply Analyst, Purchase Agent, Contract Specialist
Rhetoric and Scientific and Technical Communication	Cryptanalyst, Intelligence Specialist
Risk Management and Insurance	Program Analyst, Source Management Officer, Loan Specialist (Realty)
Russian	Foreign Languages, Intelligence Analyst, Cryptanalyst, Foreign Service Officer
Science in Agriculture	Agronomist, Agriculture Extension
Science, Technology, and Environmental Policy	Environmental Prot. Spec., Program Analyst
Scientific and Technical Communication	Technical Writer, Writer-Editor, Policy Analyst
Social Work	Social Worker, Social Psychologist, Program Analyst, Management Analyst
Sociology	Victim Specialist, Grant Program Specialist
Software Engineering	Information Technology Specialist, Computer Scientist
Soil Science	Agronomist, Agriculture Extension, Entomologist, Soil Conservation, Soil Scientist

MAJOR	TARGET JOB TITLES
Spanish	Foreign Language, Center Adjudications Officer, Immigratn Specialist
Special Education—See Educational Psychology	Education Specialist
Speech and Hearing Science	Researcher
Statistics	Mathematical Statistician, Statistician, Quality Assurance Specialist, Operations Research Analyst, Economic Research Analyst
Strategic Mgt. and Org.—See Business Administration	Program Analyst, Management Analyst
Supply Chain Management	Supply Analyst, Logistics Management Specialist
Toxicology	Toxicologist, Chemist
Transportation	Program Specialist, Logistics Management Specialist
Urban and Community Forestry	Sylviculturist, Environmental Protection Specialist
Urban and Regional Planning	Natural Conservation Resource Specialist, Environ. Protection Specialist
Veterinary Medicine	Veterinarian
Water Resources Science	Natural Conservation Resource Specialist, Environ. Protection Specialist
Wildlife Conservation	Wildlife Biologist, Animal Scientist

Conclusion

Be sure to check out *www.tenstepsforstudents.org* for federal job-related news and hot tips. The years following Presidential elections are often rife with change. But no matter who is in office, there is definitely room for you; the federal government hires an average of 300,000 new employees each year to replace workers who transfer, retire, or otherwise leave federal service, as well as creating new positions.

Internships, Summer Jobs, Scholarships & Special Programs

Ravi Nair
M.S. Computer Science
Federal Bureau of Investigation

I've always been a bit of a computer geek. At an early age, I had already rebuilt several machines for myself and my friends. I continually have spare computer parts lying around the basement, and am always concerned about their safety. (Is it too hot? What if the basement floods?) My girlfriend has to step over them, and isn't always amused.

For me, a job in Computer Science with the government is an excellent way to secure a good salary and a stable job. Additionally, working in national security will allow me to continually challenge myself in the field and stay current with emerging and new technologies.

Read more about Ravi Nair's Federal Job Search Story on the CD-ROM.

A federal internship can be your ticket to a federal career.

The federal government has a tremendous number of employment opportunities aimed at every student level from high school through post-doctorate. Many other programs in this broad category are aimed at recent graduates. Our task in this step is to provide you with an overview of these opportunities. With the information we provide, it will be your task to find which of them, if any, is right for you.

Perhaps the single most important thing to remember about these government employment opportunities is deadline. Federal hiring opportunities aimed at students often have application deadlines, and they may be many months in advance of the work start date. Some, especially internships, may require security clearances, which can take anywhere from four months to one year to perform. You should start your research process early to allow time to find opportunities, fill out applications and, if necessary, gather letters of recommendation or undergo a background check.

The second most important thing to remember about federal internships is that many opportunities the government calls internships are actually jobs. The federal government often uses the word "internship" as an umbrella term. It may refer to tuition reimbursement programs or paid, full-time, year-long positions which offer training and opportunities for permanent placement. Internships can be your ticket to a job in the federal government because the application process for many intern programs is exempt from normal competitive hiring regulations. We'll discuss this point later when we describe some of the programs that fit this description.

Let's look at some of the different employment opportunities you can explore during this step in your search for a federal job. The following box shows the variety of programs you can consider. We'll divide them into categories for you below, and discuss them in the order that they are listed in the box.

Federal Internship and Fellowship Programs

1. Apprenticeships
2. Student Employment Programs
    • Student Career Experience Program (SCEP)
    • Student Temporary Experience Program (STEP)
3. Student Volunteers
4. Scholarships
5. Grants
6. Fellowships
7. Internships
    • Presidential Management Fellowship Program
    • Federal Career Intern

Apprenticeships

Traditionally, apprenticeships have applied to skilled crafts and trades occupations, generally referred to as trades or blue-collar jobs. The government does have an apprentice program for trades (or wage grade) occupations, and we'll tell you about it.

This is a possible career path appropriate for high school graduates interested in pursuing a career in crafts or skilled trades work. These apprenticeships lead to crafts and trades jobs. While the number of federal trades jobs is shrinking, replacements for them are still needed. Apprentice programs vary by agency and location.

When used, federal crafts and trades apprenticeships operate as formal programs, combining theory and practice in the work to be performed. Completion of the program qualifies the individual as a journeyman in the field of apprenticeship, such as electrician or carpenter. Applicants for these federal apprenticeships follow normal competitive employment processes, including taking a test. Successful completion of an apprenticeship is often equivalent to a two-year degree, and qualifies the individual for the career

field without further education. Federal trades employees are paid at least as much as, and often more than, their privately employed, unionized counterparts, and usually have better benefits packages. Fully competent federal trades employees have salary growth as journeymen and promotion potential into work leader and supervisor jobs, including foreman positions. As the federal crafts and trades workforce has shrunk in recent years, many of its members have also transitioned from the wage grade to the professional (GS) workforce, often in technical positions.

You can search for federal trade apprenticeship opportunities on the USAJobs web site or on agency web sites (look particularly at the armed forces departments—especially Navy and the departments of Agriculture, the Interior, Veterans Affairs, and the General Services Administration).

Professional and Technical Apprenticeships

Federal agencies have developed several apprentice opportunities for Professional and Technical occupations. Some of these programs are very limited in their geographic or organizational reach. They cover both high school and college students. Information about these programs is available at the following web site: http://www.studentjobs.gov/d_appren.asp. You can also reach it by starting at the StudentJobs.gov site (http://www.studentjobs.gov/), and go to e-scholar then click on "Apprenticeships."

Minority High School Apprenticeship Program (MHSAP) at the Brookhaven National Laboratory.
This 4-week program is designed to stimulate 9th and 10th grade students of African, Hispanic/Latino, Native American or Pacific Islander ancestry, who have demonstrated excellence in science-oriented studies and activities. Master high school teachers and assistants mentor students in classroom and laboratory experiments.

Research and Engineering Apprenticeship Program (REAP):
This program encourages economically and socially disadvantaged high school students to pursue careers in math, science, and technology through hands-on experience in research and development. With grants from the U.S. Army, the program is administered by the Academy of Applied Science and sponsors about 120 students at 52 colleges and universities nationwide each year.

Summer High School Apprenticeship Research Program (SHARP):
This is a research-based mentorship program for high school students specifically designed to:
1. Attract and increase underrepresented students' participation and success rates in mathematics and science-related courses.
2. Encourage career paths that help build a pool of underrepresented science and engineering professionals in the work place.

U.S. Navy Science and Engineering Apprenticeship Program (SEAP):
This program provides high school and undergraduate students with the opportunity to be exposed to state-of-the-art Navy projects and programs. The participants receive an educational grant for their participation.

Q&A with Beth Ann Ritter, recent hire, Government Accountability Office

Interning on the Hill

I've always been pretty proactive when it comes to exploring all of my options and figuring out my choices. I tried to apply to jobs using all the different avenues and then taking what came my way.

The most important advice I can give is twofold: Make sure you contact your Career Services office and make certain that your resume is correct. It needs to showcase your talents and may need to be edited and re-edited. Career Services people can review your application and provide you with insights on what employers are trying to find. These experts also may draw out things in your background that you might not have considered including.

One resume or application for all the jobs is not going to cut it. You have to take the time to tailor your resume to fit each of your targeted positions.

Mistakes to avoid:

If you want to apply for jobs on the Hill, do it in two days! Go to the Senate on one day and the House on the other rather than trying to hand deliver resumes all in one day! The real key is being proactive and staying on it.

You can't just say, "I'm perfect for that job and it's going to come through." You need to apply for any job that appears to utilize your skills, even if it's not something you're super-interested in. You may find out in the interview that the job is much cooler than it sounded in the description! Or, you may get the job you wanted and find out it's not right for you.

Student Employment Programs

The federal government has two primary student employment programs—the Student Career Experience Program (SCEP) and the Student Temporary Experience Program (STEP). Both programs provide financial assistance to high school, vocational school, undergraduate and graduate students who are enrolled in school at least half-time. Depending on the agency, you may work during the summer or during the school year.

Student Temporary Experience Program (STEP) positions are much like part-time jobs. They give you and the agency maximum flexibility since the work you perform does not have to be directly related to your academic or career goals. Jobs through this program do not imply any employment commitment when you complete or leave school.

Student Career Experience Program (SCEP) differs from the STEP in significant ways. Most notably, SCEP jobs provide work experience directly related to your academic program and career goals. This program requires a written agreement involving the employing agency, the academic institution, and the student. Some colleges and universities are unwilling to enter into these agreements, so, if you are interested in this program, check early with your college placement office and the head of your academic department to make sure the school will support you. An agency may convert students in the SCEP to permanent, term, career, or career-conditional appointments without competition once the student completes his/her academic and work experience requirements. Conversion is solely at the agency's discretion.

Students in the SCEP gain exposure to public service, learn about the work of an agency, and get real-world experience in their career fields. Agencies can discover first-hand the abilities of a potential permanent employee. Once students complete their educational requirements, managers can choose to offer conversion to permanent employment based on their evaluations of students' performance in real work situations.

The federal government's student programs benefit both agencies and students. Through both programs students can learn about the working world, how to balance their time between school and work, and about flexible

work schedules and assignments. Meanwhile, agencies get work done and groom potential permanent employees.

You can learn more about these programs through OPM's web site: *http://www.opm.gov/employ/students/index.asp*. Or you may go to OPM's main web page (*http://www.opm.gov*), click on the letter S under "Site Index" in the lower right side of the main screen, and then scroll to "Students." You can then select and click on "Student Educational Experience Program" or the other student programs listed there.

To check on jobs available under student employment programs, go to the StudentJobs.gov site (*http://www.studentjobs.gov*) maintained by OPM and sponsored jointly with the U.S. Department of Education. While there you can also post your resume, sign up for notification of available opportunities, and apply for various jobs including ones available through STEP and SCEP. There is also a link to the StudentJobs.gov site from USAJobs site (*http://www.usajobs.opm.gov*). Look early and often for these opportunities, and be mindful of deadlines!

Student Volunteers

OK, you're right. "Volunteer" means without pay. Maybe that isn't for you. But if you've ever wanted to gain experience in a particular career field, or have been curious about what it's like to work for a particular federal agency, this is an opportunity for you to consider. If nothing else, it will give you the chance to have something to put in that "experience" block of your resume when you go after paying jobs.

In general, federal agencies are not allowed to accept volunteer work. But there are certain exceptions to that legal prohibition. One of the exceptions is "employment of students to further their educational goals." And a few agencies, such as the National Park Service and the Forest Service, have special permission to accept unpaid workers for specific jobs or functions. Many federal agencies offer volunteer work to high school and college students. If you are curious about a particular agency or career field, or just want to get a feel for working for a federal agency, contact the agency or agencies that interest you.

The range of volunteer possibilities is astounding. You could be involved in professional projects or other work activities related to what you are studying. Considering how diverse the federal government is, it isn't too hard to realize you could work on anything from new administrative procedures to congressional relations to issues dealing with the environment or wildlife management. The actual work assignments performed by student volunteers is determined by the host agency.

You are eligible for student volunteer work if you are enrolled at least half-time in—
  • an accredited high school or trade school
  • a technical or vocational school
  • a junior or community college
  • a four-year college or university, or
  • any other accredited educational institution.

Don't hesitate to call an agency or individual directly and ask about opportunities for student volunteer work. Be ready to sell yourself, fax over your resume, and speak about your specific interests and goals.

Scholarships

An amazing number of federal organizations offer scholarships. You can learn about these opportunities on the following web site: _http://www.studentjobs.gov/d_scholarship.asp_, or go to the _StudentJobs.gov_ website. Click on e-scholars, then on the "Scholarships" button. At the time we gathered this information, 44 different scholarship opportunities were listed there. Some focus on minority or disadvantaged students, some are for graduate of postgraduate work, and some require entering the armed forces of our country. Look here for possible funding sources for your education.

Grants

The StudentJobs.gov web site also has a button for grants. You can go directly to the grants site by going to _http://www.studentjobs.gov/d_grants.asp_. Grants are an especially important opportunity for students conducting specialized research, which often means students pursuing advanced degrees.

Numerous possibilities are presented at this site, but they aren't likely to apply to you unless you are a graduate student involved in one of the fields of study for which a grant is available, or unless you are also a career professional working for an advocacy group that could apply for one of the grants. Look here if you are curious, but most of you won't want to spend much time here.

Fellowships

The number of fellowships available through government sources is surprising, but most of these are aimed at graduate or postgraduate studies. If you are interested, go to this web site: *http://www.studentjobs.gov/d_ fellowship.asp*. Alternatively, go to the StudentJobs.gov web site and click on the "Fellowships" button. Maybe you will see something there that would interest one of your professors or parents!

Fellowships are usually federally-funded research or study opportunities. They vary widely. Some fellowships operate like scholarship funds (or grants) with academic requirements but no actual job in government. Other fellowships are like traditional jobs, many with a mentoring aspect. They may last for weeks or years. Many fellowships are offered through colleges or universities. Your school may be partially or entirely responsible for reviewing applications and awarding fellowships. In addition to the StudentJobs.gov web site link, check agency web sites and your academic department for more information.

Internships

More than 100 different intern programs are identified in the following web site: *http://www.studentjobs.gov/d_internship.asp*. You can also reach this site through the "Internship" button on the StudentJobs.gov web site. Many of these are paid; some are open only to faculty. It is worth looking at this list because it includes opportunities to serve as interns in some really neat organizations. Have you ever wanted to intern at the CIA? Check out the opportunities.

We want to focus your attention on two very special intern programs included in the lengthy list at this web site. These are special intern programs that can (and usually do) lead to permanent federal jobs. That makes them different from almost all the other internships and fellowships—or other work opportunities—included in this step. The two intern programs are the:

- Presidential Management Fellows Program (formerly known as the presidential Management Intern Program), and the
- Federal Career Intern Program

Let's look at them closely, because you may want to explore them in some depth.

Presidential Management Fellows Program

The Presidential Management Fellows Program has been around since 1977. Presidential Management Fellowships are open to graduate students (master's and doctoral-level). This program is intended to "attract to the federal service outstanding men and women from a variety of academic disciplines and career paths who have a clear interest in, and commitment to, excellence in the leadership and management of public policies and programs."

Presidential Management Fellowships are highly sought after and highly competitive. Successful applicants are appointed at GS-9. (Learn more about the GS-9 level in Step 4). They stay in the program for two years, (they may stay a third year with OPM approval), and upon completion of their Intern Program, if offered a permanent job, may be appointed at GS-12. During their two-year internship they receive rotational assignments and training opportunities intended to broaden their experience in managing and leading public programs and policies. It often is a fast track to higher jobs, including ones in the Senior Executive Service. Presidential Management Fellowships are offered only following a competitive process administered by graduate programs or professional schools. Applicants must be sponsored by their academic institutions. Each school or program has its own "nominating coordinator"; often a dean of a school. Be aware that deadlines may vary by school.

Focus on the Presidential Management Fellows Program

An overview of the application process:

1. The application process begins at the college or university, where qualified students must get past the hurdle of their schools' nomination process. Check with your school's nominating officials (e.g., dean, chair, PMF program director) to learn about its PMF nomination process. Generally, applicants may apply only during the year they will complete and satisfy all graduate degree requirements.

2. Nominees complete an application that includes an "Accomplishment Record." The completed application is submitted to the school's nominating officials.
   If the school nominates the student, PMF Program Coordinator then sends out an e-mail to the nominee, including information on the next step in the application process.

3. Nominees' Accomplishment Records are then examined, rated and ranked by an assessment panel in the PMF Program. Individuals who make it over this hurdle become semi-finalists.

4. Semi-finalists attend a one-day structured assessment process during January and February where they are rated and ranked to become finalists.

5. All finalists subsequently are invited to attend a one-day job fair in Washington, D.C. At this job fair, they and interested agencies seek to make matches. Agency representatives often have short lists of finalists they hope to offer PMF jobs, just as finalists may have agencies where they would like to work. A lot of the burden is on the finalists to make connections and pass out their resumes.

6. Once finalists are offered and accept a job, they may be appointed as Presidential Management Fellows by December 31. Finalists must complete all their academic requirements by August 31 before appointment is made.

Q&A with James Wilson, Former Director of the Presidential Management Fellows Program

On the Job Fair...

The people who tend to do better in the program are people who have higher comfort levels with ambiguity. We hand-hold applicants all the way to the job fair. But then at the job fair, we let you go! We do not set up appointments for you or tell you how to create a strategy.

You are trying to find agencies while the agencies are trying to find you. You may talk to the #1 agency on your list while you are #6 on theirs. You are waiting for them to make you an offer, but they may want to talk to five other people first. Meanwhile, another agency may have you first on their list and ready to give you an offer. I was a PMF myself and for me, I was like a kid in a candy shop. But that type of environment may be better for people who can handle it.

On the Accomplishment Record...

We are looking for demonstrated competencies, not theoretical beliefs or philosophies. If we ask applicants to write about their leadership skills, it is best if they tell us specifically what it is that they've actually done rather than their leadership philosophy.....We're asking them to demonstrate for us very clearly and succinctly—because they only get a few paragraphs—what they've done and what the results were. We are looking for results!

On Interviewing...

We're brought up to think about team, WE did this and WE did that..., because no one wants to seem like a maverick. But in this case, we're looking for the "I." We know you were a part of a team. We know you didn't reduce the deficit by yourself! But if you've been a significant component of that team you want to say so.

Federal Career Intern Program

This program was created in 2000 to give agencies flexibility to establish agency-specific programs "to provide for the recruitment and selection of exceptional employees for careers in the public sector." Given this goal, The Federal Career Intern Program can be viewed as an agency-managed version of the Presidential Management Fellow Program.

Agencies wishing to hire under this program must establish two-year programs designed to provide work experiences and training opportunities consistent with the agency's needs and the intern's competencies and career interests. Agencies typically hire persons into these intern positions at grades 5, 7, or 9, but may establish higher entry grades with OPM approval. Federal Career Internships are limited to two years unless OPM approves an extension of up to one additional year. Upon successful completion of the internship, individuals may be converted from their intern positions to competitive, permanent positions without further competition. Conversion is at the discretion of the agency. Almost any professional or administrative job important to an agency can be filled through this program.

This program is increasingly being used by federal agencies, but their individual programs are not always well defined. And no agency seems to use the term Federal Career Internship when describing or defining its job opportunities under the program. Instead, they are free to—and do—give their programs names of their own choosing that promote their purpose of the program.

An excellent example of an agency's Federal Career Intern Program initiative is the "Emerging Leaders Program" established by the Department of Health and Human Services. We strongly encourage you to examine this program's description as it appears on the department's web site. To get to the program's description, start with the DHHS web site (*http://www.dhhs.gov/*), which is not as easy to navigate as we would like. Once on the DHHS main page:

• Click the "About HHS" button at the right bottom of the screen.
• Click the "Employment" button in the column in the middle of the page.
• Click the "HHS Emerging Leaders Program" button on the left side of the page.

Voila! You have several screens of information concerning this wonderful program. One even tells you how to apply. And we're sure you won't miss noting that the department has other buttons on the left side of the screen you reached just before you started reading about the Emerging Leaders Program. Among these is their information about the Presidential Management Fellows Program and their program for developing future Senior Executives. We wish all departments and large agencies would provide such useful and informative information!

Conclusion

Finding a great internship, summer jobs, scholarships, or other special hiring opportunity is just like finding a great permanent job—it requires creativity, perseverance, and above all, planning. If you miss deadlines for opportunities you especially wanted, you may need to take an unpaid position and work part-time for a while. An internship is an irreplaceable advantage when you apply for permanent positions. So are some of the other opportunities we have identified in this step.

On the following pages we provide web site and job opportunities information for many federal departments and independent agencies. This list may not include every possible site, and agencies have a way of changing their web site addresses, but it was accurate when we did our research.

Departments of Government and Internship Information

1. Department of Agriculture www.usda.gov

> Internships & resources for College Students:
> http://www.usda.gov/da/employ/college-students.htm

> Internships & resources for Recent Grads & Experienced Professionals:
> http://www.usda.gov/da/employ/RCG&EP.htm

> Internships & resources w/ USDA for Graduate Students:
> http://www.usda.gov/da/employ/graduate.htm

2. Center for Medicare & Medicaid www.cms.gov
Fellowships & Student Employment Opportunities:
http://www.cms.gov/careers/programs/default.asp

3. Center for Medicare & Medicaid www.cms.gov
Special Programs for Students and Internships:
http://www.cms.gov/careers/programs/default.asp

4. Dept. of Commerce www.commerce.gov
Internships & Student Employment Opportunities:
http://ohrm.doc.gov/jobs/Student/info.htm

5. Dept. of Defense www.dod.mil
Internships & Student Employment Opportunities:
http://www.dod.mil/policy/isa/internships.html

6. Dept. of Education www.ed.gov/index.jhtml
Internships & Resources for College Students:
http://www.ed.gov/students/prep/job/intern/index.html?exp=0
(There is a "Note to All Prospective Interns" link & a "Student Volunteer Fact Sheet" link
along with the application on this site.)

7. Dept. of Energy www.energy.gov
Employment Opportunities:
http://www.energy.gov/engine/content.do?BT_CODE=AD_C
Career Intern Program:
http://www.ma.mbe.doe.gov/pers/Cip/applicant/index_applicant.htm

8. Dept. of Health & Human Services www.hhs.gov
Internships & Student Employment Opportunities:
http://www.hhs.gov/careers/students.html

9. Dept. of Homeland Security www.dhs.gov/dhspublic/
Employment Opportunities:
http://www.dhs.gov/dhspublic/display?theme=40
Fellowships & Internships
http://www.orau.gov/dhsed/

10. Dept. of Housing & Urban Development www.hud.gov
Internships & Student / Recent Grad Employment Opportunities:
http://www.hud.gov/offices/adm/jobs/internship.cfm

11. Dept. of the Interior www.doi.gov
Career Internships for Recent Grads:
http://www.doi.gov/doijobs/employ5.html

12. Dept. of Justice www.usdoj.gov
Internships & Student / Recent Grad Employment Opportunities:
http://www.usdoj.gov/careers/student_programs.html

13. Dept. of Labor www.dol.gov
Internships & Student Employment Opportunities:
http://www.dol.gov/_sec/media/internprogram.htm

14. Dept. of State www.state.gov
Internships & Student Employment Opportunities:
http://www.careers.state.gov/student/prog.html

15. Dept. of Transportation www.dot.gov
Employment Opportunities:
http://dothr.ost.dot.gov/Employment_Opportunities/employment_opportunities.html
Internships & Student Employment Opportunities:
http://careers.dot.gov/stuoop.html

16. Dept. of the Treasury www.treasury.gov
Employment Opportunities:
http://www.ustreas.gov/organization/employment/
Career Internships for Recent Grads:
http://www.treas.gov/offices/management/dcfo/procurement/training/

17. Dept. of Veterans Affairs www.va.gov
Employment Opportunities:
http://www.va.gov/jobs/
Internships & Student Employment Opportunities:

Independent U.S. Agencies

18. *CIA www.odci.gov*
    Internships & Student Employment Opportunities:
    http://www.odci.gov/employment/student.html

19. *Commission on Civil Rights www.usccr.gov*
    Internships & Student Employment Opportunities:
    http://www.usccr.gov/jobs/jobs.htm

20. *Commodities Future Trading Commission www.cftc.gov*
    Employment Opportunities:
    http://www.cftc.gov/ohr/ohrcareers.htm

21. *Consumer Product Safety Commission www.cpsc.gov*
    Special Programs for Students & Employment Opportunities:
    http://www.cpsc.gov/about/hr.html

22. *Corporation for National & Community Service www.cns.gov*
    Internships, Fellowships, Student Employment Opportunities:
    http://www.cns.gov/jobs/index.html

23. *Defense Nuclear Facilities Safety Board www.dnfsb.gov*
    Employment Opportunities:
    http://www.dnfsb.gov/employment/index.html
    Special Program for Recent Grads:
    http://www.dnfsb.gov/employment/employ_pdp.html

24. *Environmental Protection Agency www.epa.gov*
    Internships, Fellowships, & Student Employment Opportunities:
    http://www.epa.gov/epahome/intern.htm

25. *Equal Employment Opportunity Commission www.eeoc.gov*
    Employment Opportunities:
    http://www.eeoc.gov/soars/index.html
    Special Programs for Law Students
    http://www.eeoc.gov/soars/jobs-honor.html

26. *Export-Import Bank of the US www.exim.gov*
    Employment Opportunities:
    http://www.exim.gov/about/jobs/jobs.html

27. *Farm Credit Administration www.fca.gov*
    Employment Opportunities:
    http://www.fca.gov/careersatfca.htm

28. *Federal Bureau of Investigations* www.fbi.gov
Internship Opportunities:
http://www.fbijobs.com/intern.asp

29. *Federal Communications Commission* www.fcc.gov
Internship & Student Employment Opportunities:
http://www.fcc.gov/oig/oiginternships.html

30. *Federal Deposit Insurance Corporation* www.fdic.gov
Student Employment Opportunities:
http://www.fdic.gov/about/jobs/stuemp.html
Career Internships for Recent Grads:
http://www.fdic.gov/about/jobs/intern/index.html

31. *Federal Election Commission* www.fec.gov
Employment Opportunities:
http://www.fec.gov/jobs.htm

32. *Federal Emergency Management Agency* www.fema.gov
Employment Opportunities:
http://www.fema.gov/career/index.jsp

33. *Federal Housing Finance Board* www.fhfb.gov
Employment Opportunities:
http://www.fhfb.gov/CareerOps/Jobs.htm

34. *Federal Labor Relations Authority* www.flra.gov
Employment Opportunities:
http://www.flra.gov/29-jobs.html

35. *Federal Maritime Commission* www.fmc.gov
Employment Opportunities:
http://www.fmc.gov/jobs/jobs.htm

36. *Federal Mediation & Conciliation Service* www.fmcs.gov
Employment Opportunities:
http://www.fmcs.gov/internet/itemDetail.asp?categoryID=41&itemID=17625

37. *Federal Reserve Board* www.federalreserve.gov
Employment Opportunities:
http://www.federalreserve.gov/careers/
Internship & Student Employment Opportunities:
http://www.federalreserve.gov/careers/info.cfm?WhichCategory=8

38. Federal Retirement Thrift Investment Board _www.frtib.gov_
Employment Opportunities:
http://www.frtib.gov/personnel/index.html

39. Federal Trade Commission _www.ftc.gov_
Internships & Student Employment Opportunities:
http://www.ftc.gov/ftc/oed/hrmo/jobops.htm

40. General Services Administration _www.gsa.gov_
Employment Opportunities:
http://www.gsa.gov/GSAjobsearch

41. Institute of Museum & Library Services _www.imls.gov_
Internships & Employment Opportunities:
_http://www.imls.gov/about/abt_empl.htm_

42. Inter-American Foundation _www.iaf.gov_
Internship Opportunities:
_http://www.iaf.gov/about_iaf/iaf_jobs_en.asp?job_id=123_

43. International Broadcasting Bureau _www.ibb.gov_
Internship Opportunities:
http://www.voa.gov/interns/

44. Merit Systems Protection Board _www.mspb.gov_
Employment Opportunities:
http://www.mspb.gov/business/humanresource.html

45. National Aeronautics and Space Administration _www.nasa.gov_
Internships & Student Employment Opportunities:
_http://www.nasajobs.nasa.gov/stud_opps/index.htm_

46. National Archives & Records Administration _www.archives.gov_
Internship opportunities:
_http://www.archives.gov/careers/internships/about_internships.html_

47. National Capital Planning Commission _www.ncpc.gov_
Employment Opportunities:
http://www.ncpc.gov/about/jobs/jobs.html

48. National Credit Union Administration _www.ncua.gov_
Employment Opportunities:
http://www.ncua.gov/AboutNcua/vacancies/vacancies.html

49. *National Endowment for the Arts* www.nea.gov
    Internship Opportunities:
    http://www.nea.gov/about/Jobs/Internships.html

50. *National Endowment for the Humanities* www.neh.gov
    Employment Opportunities:
    http://www.neh.gov/whoweare/jobs.html
    Internships for Law Students:
    http://www.neh.gov/whoweare/legalinternship.html

51. *National Labor Relations Board* www.nlrb.gov
    Internships and Student Employment Opportunities:
    http://www.nlrb.gov/nlrb/about/careers/student.asp

52. *National Science Foundation* www.nsf.org
    Employment Opportunities:
    http://www.nsf.gov/oirm/hrm/jobs/start.htm
    Special Programs for Students and Recent Grads:
    http://www.nsf.gov/oirm/hrm/jobs/special.htm#scholar
    Students Employment Opportunities:
    http://www.nsf.gov/oirm/hrm/jobs/student.htm

53. *National Transportation Safety Board* www.ntsb.gov
    Internship opportunities:
    http://www.ntsb.gov/Vacancies/descriptions/Internships.htm

54. *Nuclear Regulatory Commission* www.nrc.gov
    Internships and Student Employment Opportunities:
    http://www.nrc.gov/who-we-are/employment/student-prog.html

55. *Office of Government Ethics* www.usoge.gov
    Employment Opportunities:
    http://www.usoge.gov/pages/about_oge/other_info.html

56. *Office of Personnel Management* www.opm.gov
    Employment & Student Opportunities:
    http://www.opm.gov/Career_Opportunities/index.asp

57. *Office of Special Counsel* www.osc.gov
    Internships and Student Employment Opportunities:
    http://www.osc.gov/oscjobs.htm

58. *Overseas Private Investment Corporation* www.opic.gov
    Internships and Student Employment Opportunities:
    http://www.opic.gov; Click on Employment, then Internship Program

59. *Peace Corps www.peacecorps.gov*
Internship & Fellowship Opportunities:
http://www.peacecorps.gov/index.cfm?shell=resources.grads

60. *Pension Benefit Guaranty Corporation www.pbgc.gov*
Employment Opportunities:
http://www.pbgc.gov/about/jobopps.htm

61. *Postal Rate Commission www.prc.gov*
Employment Opportunities:
http://www.prc.gov/main.asp; Click on Employment

62. *Social Security Administration www.ssa.gov*
Student & Recent Grad Employment Opportunities:
http://www.ssa.gov/careers/students&grads.htm
Internship Opportunities:
http://www.ssa.gov/policy/jobs/intern.htm

63. *Securities & Exchange Commission www.sec.gov*
Internship Programs: *http://www.sec.gov/jobs.shtml#intern*

64. *Selective Services System www.sss.gov*
Employment Opportunities:
http://www.sss.gov/Job%20Opportunities.htm

65. *Small Business Administration www.sba.gov*
Employment Opportunities:
http://www.sba.gov/jobs/index.html
SBA PMI Opportunities:
http://www.sba.gov/pmi/

66. *Tennessee Valley Authority*
Internship & Student & Recent Grad Employment Opportunities:
http://www.tva.gov/employment/recruiting.htm

67. *Trade & Development Agency www.tda.gov*
Internship & Employment Opportunities:
http://www.tda.gov/abouttda/jobs.html

68. *U.S. Agency for International Development www.usaid.gov*
Internship Opportunities:
http://www.usaid.gov/careers/studentprograms.html
Internships for Law Students:
http://www.usaid.gov/careers/gcintern.html

69. United States Postal Service www.usps.com
Internship Opportunities:
http://www.usps.com/employment/internships.htm

Quasi-Official Agencies

70. Legal Services Corporation www.lsc.gov
Internship & Employment Opportunities:
http://www.lsc.gov/employ.htm

71. Smithsonian Institution www.si.edu
Internships Opportunities:
http://www.si.edu/index.html
Fellowship Opportunities:
http://www.si.edu/ofg/

72. United States Institute of Peace www.usip.org
Employment Opportunities:
http://www.usip.org/jobs/index.html

Other Helpful Resources for Students & Recent Grads

73. www.students.gov
Student gateway to the U.S. Government: Financial Aid, Career Development, Military Service, Community Service, and more

74. Presidential Management Intern Program
http://www.pmi.opm.gov/

75. White House Internship Program
www.whitehouse.gov/government/wh-intern.html

Understanding Federal Jobs: Target Your Grade and Salary

Erickson Young
BA. Government and Spanish
Peace Corps Volunteer, Peace Corps of America

My friends tell me that I am a very determined person. I guess they
have a point, as I have known that I wanted to work in public service
all my life. The photo here is of me and U.S. Senator Max Cleland
– a very important networking contact! I graduated from Gallaudet
University in Washington, D.C. with a degree in Government
and Spanish. I immediately began my search for a job in the State
Department, Immigration, or Peace Corps.

I had never searched for Federal jobs before except the temporary
Student Intern/Staff Assistant position for U.S. Senator Max
Cleland, which was not permanent. As a student, I didn't apply
for Federal jobs through vacancy announcements, so I had no
experience with writing a Federal resume or KSAs. It was a unique
experience. I worked with Gallaudet's career center director who
assisted me with the special hiring authority for people with
disabilities. I also applied competitively through announcements on
www.usajobs.opm.gov. I'm thrilled to say that I am starting my career
as a Peace Corps Volunteer in Latin America in the coming fall!

Read Erickson's entire case study on the CD-ROM.

A Quick Overview Concerning Federal Grade and Pay Structure

The federal civil service has different grading and pay structures for its professional and trade workforces. Because you are most likely a college student or graduate, we're going to focus in this step on professional jobs ranging from accountants and cryptanalysts to special agents and biologists. The government categorizes this broad group of job titles in a system called PATCO, which stands for **P**rofessional, **A**dministrative, **C**lerical, **T**echnical, and **O**ther. (See the PATCO Chart on page 52.)

The professional jobs are organized into one of 15 grades in a system called the General Schedule. General Schedule grades represent levels of difficulty and responsibility that are in fact defined by law. They are identified by the letters "GS", followed by numbers, such as GS-1 (the lowest grade) to GS-15 (the highest). A recent graduate with a bachelor's degree would usually qualify for a GS-5 or 7.

Each GS grade has an associated "base pay" range that includes a minimum and a maximum rate of pay. There are ten pay rates between the base minimum and maximum. Base pay ranges are approximate (usually lower) than actual salary, because a locality pay is added depending on the city of employment, (i.e. New York includes a locality pay). Both the base pay and locality pay are subject to adjustments each year, generally upward. Shortly we'll show you the GS base pay rates for 2004.

The GS Pay System

The ten rates for each GS grade are called "steps." Movement through steps of a grade recognizes increased skill and knowledge level in the job. This contrasts with movement between grades, which really is a promotion involving taking on new, greater duties and responsibilities and getting paid more for doing so. Movement among steps is faster at the lower end of the scale, when people are learning more about their jobs. See the general schedule pay scale on page 86.

Introducing Pay Banding Pay Schedules

Now that we have covered the basic general schedule grade and pay system, we'll tell you that not every agency follows this pay system anymore. "Pay banding," which allows an organization to combine two or more grades into a wider "band" is an increasingly popular alternate to the traditional GS system. The "grade" information for jobs in agencies using pay banding will have a different look, and that look may be specific to a particular agency. Don't be surprised to see something as odd as ZP-1 or NO-2 in place of GS-5 or GS-7. Focus on the duties, the salary, whether you are qualified for the job, and whether you would like to have it. Remember, the federal government is large, and needs a way to increase flexibility of pay based on performance. Pay bands are their answer.

Examples of Pay Band Salaries

Department of Commerce, National Institute of Standards and Technology Pay Bands

	GS 1	GS 2	GS 3	GS 4	GS 5	GS 6	GS 7	GS 8	GS 9	GS 10	GS 11	GS 12	GS 13	GS 14	GS 15
ZA Administrative			1					2			3		4		5
ZP Professional			1					2			3		4		5
ZS Support	1		2		3		4		5						
ZT Technical			1				2			3		4	5		

Navy Research Lab

	GS 1	GS 2	GS 3	GS 4	GS 5	GS 6	GS 7	GS 8	GS 9	GS 10	GS 11	GS 12	GS 13	GS 14	GS 15	GS 16+
NP Scientist & Engineer Professional			I				II					III		IV		V
NR Scientist & Engineer Technical			I				II			III	IV		V			
NO Administrative Specialist/Professional			I				II				III	IV	V			
NC Administrative Support			I			II		III								

How to Find Your Grade Level

The federal government determines your eligibility for a job at a certain grade and salary by assessing your education and experience. For many occupations experience is paramount, but education can be substituted for experience up to GS-11. If you are about to graduate from undergraduate school, then a GS-5 or possibly a GS -7 position is correct. If you are about to graduate from graduate school, you could qualify for a GS-9, while one year of graduate work could qualify you for GS-7. A Ph.D. will make you eligible for jobs at GS-11. Work experience outside of your school coursework may help in determining the highest grade for which you qualify. See the Educational Qualifications Chart below:

Educational Qualifications Chart

Qualifying Based on Education Alone

GS-2:	High school graduation or equivalent (i.e., GED)
GS-3:	One year above high school
GS-4:	Two years above high school (or Associate's Degree)
GS-5:	Bachelor's Degree
GS-7:	One full year of graduate study or Bachelor's degree with Superior Academic Achievement (There are three ways to qualify for Superior Academic Achievement. See the table below for further information.)
GS-9:	Master's Degree or equivalent such as J.D. or LL.B.
GS-11:	Ph.D. or, for research positions only, completion of all requirements for a master's or equivalent degree
GS-12:	For research positions only, completion of all requirements for a doctoral or equivalent degree

Note: All positions at or above GS-13 require appropriate specialized experience, and do not allow education to be substituted for that specialized experience.

Superior Academic Performance and Grade Adjustments

The three ways to qualify for Superior Academic Achievement designation (and thus be eligible for GS-7 as a graduate with a Baccalaureate degree)		
1.	Class standing	Must be in the upper third of your graduating class in your college, university, or major subdivision such as the School of Business.
2.	Grade-point average*	a. 3.0 out of a possible 4.0 ("B" or better) recorded on your transcript, or as computed based on 4 years of education, or as computed based on all courses completed during the final 2 years of your curriculum, or b. 3.5 or higher out of a possible 4.0 "B+" or better) based on the average of the required courses completed in the major field or the required courses in the major field completed during the final 2 years of the curriculum.
3.	Election to membership in a National Honor Society	Honor societies listed in the Association of College Honor Society of American College Fraternities (1991) meet this requirement. Membership in a freshman honor society does not meet this rquirement.

* OPM instructions say GPA should be credited in the manner most beneficial to the applicant.

The jobs you are likely to be considering will require an education beyond high school (only GS-1 jobs do not have any qualifying minimum education level), but education alone is not necessarily the deciding qualifications factor. For federal jobs in many professional and administrative occupations, experience is the paramount qualifier; education is allowed to substitute for experience. Thus you can qualify for many positions with only practical experience.

Federal jobs in some occupations have a "positive education requirement," meaning you must meet specific educational requirements to be hired for them. The educational requirements may be expressed in terms of semester hours in particular fields of study (e.g., 24 hours of accounting coursework) or a specific kind of degree (e.g., a bachelor's degree in the engineering field appropriate to the engineering job being filled). Each vacancy announcement should clearly state the requirements you must meet to be qualified to compete for the job opening.

PATCO CHART

Federal jobs are made up of the following basic categories, titles, and grades:

PROFESSIONAL – GS-5 through 15
The professional positions have a POSITIVE EDUCATIONAL REQUIREMENT, including such occupations as chemist, accountant, doctor, engineer, social worker, or psychologist. Where there is an educational requirement, the education must meet standards set by the profession involved.

ADMINISTRATIVE – GS-5 through 15
These jobs usually have the title of ANALYST or SPECIALIST. You can qualify for these jobs solely on the basis of experience, but below GS-12 education can be substituted for the required experience. If you have no experience, then you need a degree to qualify for entry-level (GS-5 and 7) administrative positions. Certain law enforcement investigative and inspection positions are in this category: (Special Agent, Border Patrol, Customs Inspector, Immigration Inspector).

TECHNICAL – GS-6 through 9
These jobs are the TECHNICIAN or ASSISTANT positions, such as Accounting Technician or Assistant. Although a two- or four-year degree may be required in some fields (especially medical technician occupations), the primary qualifications requirement is experience. The Federal Aviation Administration Electronics Technician can be classified as high as a GS-12. Bachelor's degree graduates can qualify for Technician or Assistant positions starting at GS-7 with superior academic achievement.

CLERICAL – GS-1 through 5
These are the CLERK positions. There is no college degree requirement. An Associate of Arts degree graduate or two-year certification program will qualify for GS-3 or -4 positions.

OTHER
This category includes jobs that do not fit other categories. It includes many law enforcement occupations, including security guard, police, ranger, park ranger, and U.S. Marshall but does not include criminal investigators ("special agent"). Research psychologists and social scientists are also among the occupations in this category. The grades for this "Other" category can range from GS-3 to GS-15.

How to Get Promoted

Once hired, it is possible to advance to higher levels with on-the-job experience and good performance. As you explore vacancy announcements, look for ones that indicate "promotion potential" to a grade higher than the one you are immediately seeking. In fact, look for the highest promotion potential you can find. This "promotion potential" means you can be promoted to whatever grade is listed without having to compete for that promotion. This potential is the "full performance level" for the job—the grade every fully-successful person in that job in that organization can reach based on demonstrating the ability to do the job. While such promotions are not automatic (you earn them by showing growth in the job), you will achieve them if you work hard. And again, while not automatic, these noncompetitive (called "career ladder") promotions usually come after one year in each lower grade level. "Full performance levels" are determined by the hiring agency; two agencies can make different decisions regarding full performance grades for the same jobs. This is why you want to include "promotion potential" as one of the things you examine when you look at vacancy announcements.

See the career ladder vacancy announcements showing promotion in Step 5, pages 87 to 91.

If you are hired for a federal job that has no stated promotion potential, or once you reach the top promotion potential for a job, you must compete against other individuals for higher grade positions. The rules for promotion and other internal placement actions for federal employees are different from the rules that apply to you before you are hired. Generally speaking, you have a lot more opportunities once you are "inside the system." The federal government is a very large employer, but don't forget that as grades get higher, there are fewer jobs at this level (similar to an ever-steepening pyramid).

Announcement Comparison: Career Growth Potential

Example 1 - Great Career Growth Potential
Center Adjudications Officer (CAO) GS-1801-5/7 (Promotion Potential GS-12)

In this job you will start out as either a GS-5 or GS-7 and be promoted to a GS-12 without further competition while in this position. Jobs like this are excellent because they offer tremendous increases in responsibility and pay based solely on your ability to learn and grow in the job for which you are hired. In this instance, you could achieve GS-12 in four years if you start out as a GS-5, and in three years if hired as a GS-7. This is because of another oddity in the federal GS grading scheme: the even grades between GS-5 and -11 are not used for most professional or administrative occupations; instead, their normal grade progression is GS 5, -7, -9, -11, -12, -13, -14, -15.

Example 2 - No Career Growth Potential
Scheduling Analyst, GS-0301-9 Promotion Potential: None

This job offers only the GS-9 salary with no promotion potential. For someone with a Master's Degree and no work experience, GS-9 responsibilities and pay are not bad at all. But in order to be promoted, you would have to leave this job and get another one, and you would have to do this by competing for other announced vacancies. So after one year, you would update your federal resume and search for jobs at the next grade level (GS-11). You can do this because you have gained the "one year of specialized experience at GS-9" and also "one year time in grade."

When applying for federal jobs, specify the lowest grade (or pay) you are willing to receive, as the HR reviewer is prohibited from considering you for grades lower than the lowest one you state on your application. On the other hand, if you state that you will accept a certain grade (say, GS-5) and you are qualified for a higher one (GS-7 in this example), the HR reviewer may, but is not obligated to, consider you for the higher grade. This is an area where you, as the applicant, are supposed to have done your homework! Remember that the HR reviewer may be looking at hundreds of applications, and relies on you to state the grade level you are seeking. Some reviewers are more helpful than others when it comes to advising applicants. Don't rely on the one reviewing your application to do work that you can do!

Outstanding Scholar Program

There are 100 professional and administrative occupations that can hire through individuals who meet the definition of "Outstanding Scholar" without competition.

This program is widely used by some agencies and not used at all by others. Although the Outstanding Scholar Program allows agencies to hire individuals without competition, some agencies have established Outstanding Scholar hiring programs that include competition. These agencies accept applications from college graduates who meet the Outstanding Scholar definition and then make their selections based on how well the qualifications of the people in this restricted applicant pool meet their job needs.

An Outstanding Scholar is defined as someone who earned a Bachelor's Degree from an accredited school and who meets either of the following criteria:

1. Earned a 3.5 Grade Point Average or higher during their undergraduate education (3.45 also qualifies because it rounds up to 3.5), or
2. Graduated in the upper ten percent of their undergraduate class or major university subdivision, such as the College of Arts and Sciences.

The Outstanding Scholar Program does not require that the degree be recently earned, which may help explain why OPM data shows that the average age of all outstanding scholars hired in fiscal year 2000 was nearly 30 years. Neither does the Program require a specific relationship between the degree earned and the job being filled.

Most agencies clearly identify on the vacancy announcements their outstanding scholar job openings. If you meet the qualifications, this is a hiring possibility you should consider. Most hiring should be at GS-7 because Outstanding Scholars meet Superior Academic Achievement criteria, but the agency can choose to offer only GS-5. This is an agency decision, just as accepting or rejecting the terms of a job offer is yours. Agencies may accept your application before you are a graduate, but they

will require verification of your eligibility before actually hiring you. You will be required to prove you meet one of the eligibility criteria through a transcript (GPA) or certification by the appropriate School or Academic Department (top 10% requirement).

The Bilingual/Bicultural Program—Another Special Hiring Possibility to Consider

Increasingly, federal agencies find a need for employees who are bilingual or who have a good understanding of the culture of another ethnic group. The government has a special court-approved hiring program for individuals who are fluent in both Spanish and English, or who have substantial knowledge of Hispanic culture. For students or recent graduates, meeting either of these requirements may work to your advantage.

Through the Bilingual/Bicultural Program, federal agencies may hire without competition individuals who are basically qualified for the job being sought, so long as the job requires the bilingual skill (Spanish/English) or bicultural knowledge (Hispanic/Anglo) and the individual meets this requirement.

This program applies to the same group of more than 100 occupations eligible for Outstanding Scholar appointment, and applies only to hiring at the entry level (GS-5 and 7). Agencies may not always advertise in their vacancy announcements that they will hire using this special method, but **if** the job requirements include skill in Spanish and English, or knowledge of Hispanic culture; **if** the job is being filled at GS-5 or 7; and **if** the announcement is for an occupation subject to the Outstanding Scholar Program; **then** the Bilingual/Bicultural Program also applies. If you possess the special Spanish language skill or Hispanic culture knowledge, we suggest you take the initiative and ask the agency if it will consider you under the Bilingual/Bicultural Program. An agency is not required to do so, but neither is it prohibited from doing so, because the program is not subject to normal competitive hiring rules. So long as you are qualified for the job (and possession of a 4-year degree is considered "qualified" for entry-level jobs in the occupations involved), you may be selected and appointed without regard to how other applicants scored for the job. Because the language skill or cultural knowledge may be in short supply and high demand, getting a job through this program may even give you some leverage if you want to ask the agency to pay your student loan debt, give you a signing bonus, or hire you above the lowest rate for your grade.

Sorry, if you meet either program requirement in a language other than Spanish or a culture other than Hispanic, this program isn't for you.

Salary Table 2004-GS
2004 General Schedule
INCORPORATING A 2.70% GENERAL INCREASE
Effective January 2004

Annual Rates by Grade and Step
without locality adjustments

GS	1	2	3	4	5	6	7	8	9	10
1	15625	16146	16666	17183	17703	18009	18521	19039	19060	19543
2	17568	17985	18567	19060	19274	19841	20408	20975	21542	22109
3	19168	19807	20446	21085	21724	22363	23002	23641	24280	24919
4	21518	22235	22952	23669	24386	25103	25820	26537	27254	27971
5	24075	24878	25681	26484	27287	28090	28893	29696	30499	31302
6	26836	27731	28626	29521	30416	31311	32206	33101	33996	34891
7	29821	30815	31809	32803	33797	34791	35785	36779	37773	38767
8	33026	34127	35228	36329	37430	38531	39632	40733	41834	42935
9	36478	37694	38910	40126	41342	42558	43774	44990	46206	47422
10	40171	41510	42849	44188	45527	46866	48205	49544	50883	52222
11	44136	45607	47078	48549	50020	51491	52962	54433	55904	57375
12	52899	54662	56425	58188	59951	61714	63477	65240	67003	68766
13	62905	65002	67099	69196	71293	73390	75487	77584	79681	81778
14	74335	76813	79291	81769	84247	86725	89203	91681	94159	96637
15	87439	90354	93269	96184	99099	102014	104929	107844	110759	113674

The rates in the chart above are basic rates. Locality adjustments between 10.90% and 24.21% are in effect for 2004.

Conclusion

Review vacancy announcements carefully. Look for ones for which you are qualified, and that offer noncompetitive promotion several grades above the level where you will start. If you're not sure of the right level to apply for if the agency is hiring at multiple grades, do your best to apply for the correct grade level (one you qualify for). If you shoot too high and are found unqualified, your chances for that job are finished even if you are qualified for a lower grade.

After you are offered a job, you may be able to negotiate benefits like student loan payment, travel expenses, telecommuting, or sign-on bonuses. You are in a better position to negotiate if your skills are in demand. If you have highly sought-after technical or language skills, keep that potential bargaining power in mind during interviews and subsequent negotiations. Be aware of federal government job needs and new hiring trends or campaigns. More tips on Interviewing for the job are in Step 10!

Finding Vacancy Announcements for Federal Jobs & Internships

Andrea Fritchey
Information Assistant, GS-1001-05
Clear Creek Ranger District
USDA Forest Service

Growing up in Maine, I always had access to beautiful scenery
– Bar Harbor, White Mountain National Forest, state parks – and
found that I wanted to contribute to the preservation of our
national resources. (My friends call me a tree-hugger!) Just after
getting my Bachelor's in Human Ecology, I started working as a
seasonal park ranger for the U.S. Forest Service, giving tours and
providing interpretive information to visitors. I really enjoyed
working with the public and raising awareness of conservation
topics, and the diverse responsibilities of the position.

Now, as a Visitor Information Assistant with USFS Clear Creek
Ranger District, Idaho Springs, CO, I plan new programs and
develop and give presentations to school-aged children and
seniors. I also provide information to Park visitors and help
them navigate and appreciate the park. Working at the Forest
Service, it makes me feel good to know that my job enables the
public to value and protect our natural resources.

Read Andrea's Federal Resume on the CD-ROM.

1 2 3 4 **5** 6 7 8 9 10

Locating a vacancy announcement for which you are qualified can be like finding gold!

This Step will help you find and interpret vacancy announcements. We will introduce you to federal job announcements and why they are so important. We will explain the various automated application systems (there's more than one) that you will use to submit your resume. We will provide you with a list of websites that include most federal job announcements. And, we will show samples of a few agency websites that use automated systems to receive and manage federal resume applications.

You have found a great vacancy announcement when it:

- is issued by an agency and office whose mission is right for you;
- contains the job title and duties that match your interests, background and education;
- has a duty location that appeals to you; and,
- you are qualified for the grade level.

The federal government's principal vacancy announcement (job listings) website is *www.usajobs.opm.gov*. There are an average of 17,500 jobs listed on this site on any given day.

There are two critical reasons to research vacancy announcements early in the federal job search process. They are to:

- Locate and target specific jobs for which you are qualified
- Identify the "keywords" required to write an effective and successful federal resume.

Internet Research and Electronic Resumes

Do you enjoy Internet research? If the answer is YES, then you will benefit from looking for ideal jobs and internship opportunities online. Even if this approach does not thrill you, the Internet is the most effective way to find federal jobs today.

At the time this book was published, there were a number of databases to which you could submit your resume and supporting materials online to apply for government jobs. Although not all federal agencies are using automated systems to manage their job applications and assess their applicants, many are. Federal agencies have choices among several commercial and government-developed automated systems, and also are free to develop their own. Shortly, we'll give you some examples of how the main systems work. A key point to remember is that it is very, very important to read carefully the "how to apply" directions found in each vacancy announcement. Submitting an application to each database takes time and patience, and each database has unique characteristics. We will cover the "how to apply" instructions in more detail in *Step 8, Apply for Federal Jobs.*

Each federal job announcement contains specific and essential information about applying for the position(s) for which you are qualified. Announcements contain important language or "keywords," which you can use in your resume. Each agency's unique culture and mission is reflected in these descriptive words used to express the agency's requirements for the job advertised. They are found in the job announcement, typically in the "duties" and "qualifications" sections. Finding and addressing the keywords is vital to writing an effective and successful electronic federal resume.

Begin with one well-written electronic federal resume targeted toward your objective job title(s). Build your resume by responding to the keywords and phrases in the announcement with your specific skills and interests, education, and experience. With one well-written electronic federal resume, you are well on your way to a successful federal job search! You can cut and paste your resume repeatedly for additional job openings. This greatly simplifies your federal job search. You will learn how to create a well-written electronic federal resume in *Step 6, Write your Federal and Electronic Resumes.*

In addition, many vacancy announcements will require additional experience examples, or "Knowledge, Skills, and Abilities" narratives (KSAs). You will learn how to write job-winning KSAs in *Step 7, Write KSAs and Cover Letters.*

Federal Job Web Sites with Virtually all Available Jobs

www.usajobs.opm.gov – The official government site. Free.
www.avuecentral.com – Free commercial site that includes information about
   federal jobs in agencies that are using the AVUE automated system.
   (Not all federal agencies use this system.) Free.
www.fedjobs.com – Contains a good search engine. Fee charged.
www.federaljobsearch.com – Has a great geographic search engine. Fee charged.

Agency Website Job Listings

Most departments and agencies have their own job information websites
or pages. They may also provide information to the main government job
information site (*www.usajobs.opm.gov*). If you are focusing your job search
on specific agencies, register at these agencies' websites and search for jobs
within their listings. Frequently, agencies provide more information on their
own websites about jobs and how to apply for them than they include in the
announcements placed on USAJobs. Individual agency websites also include
their database registration pages for their on-line application forms.

*Agencies may list their vacancy announcements in multiple websites -- and
not every agency is required to include its vacancies on USAJobs.*

Traditional vs. Nontraditional Civil Service

Size breeds complexity! The federal government is the largest employer in
the U.S. comprised of hundreds of separate organizations. Many of these
organizations belong to the traditional civil service, and follow a common set
of hiring rules. Many others, however, lie outside the traditional civil service,
and may have their own hiring policies. To complicate things even more, one
agency may have different hiring policies within each department.

In the next section of this step we'll identify for you a number of federal
organizations that are not subject to traditional civil service rules. Keep in
mind, if you are interested in working for any of these agencies, you should
be sure to check agencies' websites to learn about vacancies.

The fact that not all vacancies are located in one place is both a challenge and an opportunity for you, the federal job seeker. It is a challenge because it suggests that you should not rely only on the USAJobs site when you look for federal jobs, but also consult homepages of federal agencies for which you might want to work. If those agencies post their jobs on USAJobs, (and most do), they should have a link to that site. If those agencies do not, they will guide you to their own recruitment webpage. You can't lose by taking this additional step. And while you are on the agency-specific site, you can learn useful information about the agency, its mission, its culture, and its jobs.

Whether or not you use Internet tools to pursue your federal job search, keep an eye open for other ways federal agencies recruit and advertise their openings. For example, they increasingly are participating in or running their own job fairs. They may recruit through school career centers, and some even use newspaper advertising. The additional means of advertising their jobs are not limited to agencies with their own hiring rules, but may be more common among them.

In the next section we provide some examples of agencies or agency components that are not subject to the entire range of civil service rules governing hiring. Some are outside the civil service because of special provisions in the laws that created them. Others are not part of the executive branch, and therefore are not part of the civil service. Whether they are part of the civil service does not determine whether these agencies post their vacancies on USAJobs, but their inclusion here is a reminder that you should check their home pages when you are conducting your federal job search.

Excepted Agencies

Transportation Security Agency, Department of Homeland Security
Federal Reserve System, Board of Governors
  Central Intelligence Agency
  Defense Intelligence Agency, Department of Defense
  Foreign Service, U.S. Department of State
  Federal Bureau of Investigation, Department of Justice
  Agency for International Development
  National Security Agency, Department of Defense
  National Imagery and Mapping Agency, Department of Defense
  U.S. Nuclear Regulatory Commission
  Post Rate Commission
  Health Services and Research Administration, Department of
  Veterans Affairs (Physicians, nurses, and allied medical personnel)

Government Corporations, such as:
  U. S. Postal Service
  Tennessee Valley Authority
  The Virgin Islands Corporation

Judicial Branch
Legislative Branch (including the Government Accountability Office)
Public International Organizations:
  International Monetary Fund
  Pan American Health Organization
  United Nations Children's Fund
  United Nations Development Program
  United Nations Institute
  United Nations Population Fund
  United Nations Secretariat
  World Bank, IFC and MIGA

Important Elements in a Vacancy Announcement:

Title of Job, Grade and Salary:

Be sure the job is right for you. Some job titles in government are unusual and not typically recognized in the employment world. However, they might be just right for you. For instance:

- **Industrial Specialist** (General), GS-1150-5/7 (Promotion Potential GS-12), Defense Contract Management Agency (This could be a good opportunity for Business majors.)
- **Center Ajudications Officer**, GS-1801-7 (Promotion Potential GS-12), Customs and Border Protection (Perhaps a good fit for International Relations, Criminal Justice, and Political Science majors.)
- **Visual Information Specialist**, GG-1084-7/9/11/12, National Ground Intelligence Center, Information Management Directorate, Visual Services Division, Charlottesville, VA (Sounds like it was made for Graphic Arts and possibly other arts majors.)
- **Program Analyst** (Governmental), SV 0343-F, G or H (Pay Bands) Department of Homeland Security, TSA (Any major might qualify. Look at the duties to learn more.)

Closing date:

If the deadline is unrealistic, it could be disastrous for you to apply for the position. This will depend on you. If you have your federal resume drafted and are ready to start applying for jobs immediately, go for it! If the closing date says "Open Continuously," "Inventory Building," or has a closing date that is far off in the future, then the organization is using this announcement to build an inventory of future job candidates. Names of qualified applicants will be placed in a database for future (and also possibly current) job openings. Such announcements represent many jobs that the agency expects to open up at any time.

Who Can Apply

"Open to Anyone With or Without Status." If the announcement says "Open to Anyone," then you can apply. "Status" refers to current federal employees and former employees whose length of previous federal employment and type of appointment qualify them for reinstatement. NOTE: Most federal civil

service jobs require U.S. citizenship, but jobs in other federal systems (such as the Postal Service, National Institutes of Health and other agencies) may not. If you are not a U.S. citizen, read this part of the announcement carefully.

Citizenship and Federal Employment

As a general rule, only U.S. citizens or nationals are eligible for competitive jobs in the civil service. This restriction was established by an executive order. In addition, Congress annually imposes a ban on using appropriated funds to hire noncitizens within the United States (certain groups of noncitizens are not included in this ban). Further, immigration law limits public and private sector hiring to only individuals who are 1) U.S. citizens or nationals; 2) aliens assigned by the U.S. Citizenship and Immigration Services (CIS) to a class of immigrants authorized to be employed (the largest group in this class is aliens lawfully admitted for permanent U.S. residence), or 3) an individual alien expressly authorized by the CIS to be employed.

Despite all of these limitations and restrictions, it is possible for noncitizens to obtain federal jobs in the U.S. For example, an agency may hire a qualified noncitizen in the excepted service or the Senior Executive Service if it is permitted to do so by the annual appropriations act and immigration law. And, if agencies cannot find qualified citizens to fill jobs in the competitive service, they may then hire noncitizens for those jobs. However, noncitizens may only be given an excepted appointment and will never acquire "status." They may not be promoted or reassigned to another civil service job except in situations where qualified citizens are not available.

Office
The office where the job is located is very important. The office title will help identify the mission of the job. For example, it could be Information Technology, Legal Services, Policy and Planning, or EEO.

Location/Duty Station

Make sure you are willing to work in the geographic location of the position you are seeking. When hiring new employees, federal agencies must accept applications regardless of where the applicant lives. (For example, an agency must accept an application from a person living in Florida who seeks a job in Alaska). However, the agency may refuse to pay moving and relocation expenses. Read the announcement carefully to find out what your obligations are.

Knowledge, Skills, and Abilities, or KSAs (which may also be identified as "competencies")

Read the announcement carefully to see if KSA narratives will be required to be written on separate sheets of paper, or if the KSAs can be described in the text of your resume. (See Chapter 7 for more instruction on KSA writing.)

Duties

Always read the duties carefully because the title of the position may not accurately reflect the duties of the job. The duties could represent a completely different job than the one you thought would be described. Sometimes government job titles just do not match the duties you would expect.

Qualifications

Read the required qualifications to determine if you have the generalized and specialized experience, or have education that can substitute for it. If the announcement uses the term "one year," that means 52 weeks, 40 hours per week. Relevant experience gained from part-time jobs can be combined to determine how much job-related experience you have. If the hours combine to make one year of specialized experience, then you can be credited with that year. For many jobs, qualifications are expressed in terms of experience or education, or combinations of the two. Possession of a Bachelor's Degree is often enough to qualify someone for an entry-level (GS-5 or sometimes GS-7) job in many professional or administrative occupations—the type of jobs most graduates seek following college.

For career changers returning to college for another degree, you may qualify for your new career as a GS-5, 7, 9 based on your education alone. You will probably have to move back in your earnings, but you can move ahead in your new career.

"One year of specialized experience" means that you have one year of experience that is specialized in this work and at this level. One year in the federal HR world is equal to 52 weeks at 40 hours per week. If you held four internships over a period of two years and worked 20 hours per week, in a specialized field, you would have one year of specialized experience.

How to Apply

Read the instructions to determine what to send with your application and which resume format to use. Sometimes this is not clear. While most agencies now use an online application system that takes you step-by-step through the application process, many still do not. The burden is squarely on the applicant to submit a complete, accurate application in a timely manner. If you are going to take the time to apply for a federal job, be sure you submit a complete application! See Step 8 for more details on "How to Apply."

Types of Job Announcements

Job Announcements with Specific Closing Dates:
These announcements are for positions that are being recruited for specifically. Timing for response could be as little as a couple of days or as long as several weeks. Agencies set these dates based on their experience with the relevant job markets.

Open Inventory – Standing Registers – Database Announcements:
These are announcements for jobs that are continually being recruited for or when a future need for candidates is anticipated. The closing dates could be far into the future, or there may be none. The names of qualified applicants are stored in a database, and the HR staff will search the database when a supervisor requests a person meeting the job's requirements. Timing for filling jobs covered by this kind of announcement is an unknown, so you may be in for a long wait if you respond to one. But you could be pleasantly surprised by the speed with which the agency offers you a job. What is certain is that if you do not have your resume in the database, you won't get considered at all.

Closing Date Announcement:

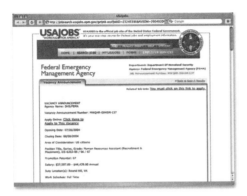

Standing Register Announcement:

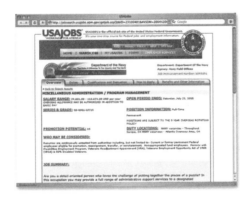

Federal Job Websites:

Office of Personnel Management Official Jobs Website
www.usajobs.opm.gov or *www.usajobs.com*

This is the Office of Personnel Management's main website for federal jobs. It is free of charge and quite easy to use.

Search Recommendation No. 1: Search ALL JOBS

Go to the Agency Search (a top link)
Search for:

Department:	Select All
Location Search:	Select All (or select your state)
Series No:	Leave Blank
Occupational Series:	Select All (or search for a job, but that will greatly narrow your results)
Salary Range:	$25,000 to $40,000 for GS-5 to 7 (entry-level jobs)
Applicant Eligibility:	Click NO if you have not worked for the government before and have not had military experience or any of the choices above this selection
Sort:	By date
View Description:	Detailed
Results:	U.S.-Wide, 3,565 jobs came up that are in this grade and salary level!

This search will present all of the job titles in this geographic area within this salary range. You can review the job titles and duties to determine if the jobs are of interest to you. It is important to search for ALL JOBS because federal job titles are not as straightforward as we would like, and they are prone to change as new job needs arise in agencies. If you limit your job search to a particular job title with which you are familiar, you may not learn about all of the job openings for which you are qualified—or even those that represent your particular field of interest. For instance, would you automatically think to search for Program Specialist or Management Analyst? Surprisingly, these popular government job titles mean many things. The range of program possibilities is phenomenal - environmental, food and nutrition, transportation, education, health, health insurance, homeland security. You name it, the government probably has a program specialist or management analyst working on it!

EXAMPLE
>   Position: Program Specialist
>   GS-0301-09/11
>   Promotion Potential GS-11
> $43,139 - $67,852 Per Annum
>   Career/Career Conditional Appointment
>   Multiple Full-time Permanent Positions

Searching for Grade Levels: GS-0301-09/11
If you are a BA/BS graduate, then you should search for GS-5 to 7 announcements. If you have a 3.25 cumulative GPA or above, you may qualify as a GS-7 to start.

If you are an advanced degree graduate or have one year specialized experience, you can begin your search at GS-9.

If you are a two-year college graduate or technical training school graduate, then you would search for jobs at the GS-3 to 4 range - based on your training.

If you are a high school student, you can search for student jobs at the grade levels GS-2 and 3.

Promotion Potential to GS-11. The "Promotion Potential" block indicates the highest grade to which you can be promoted without further competition or applying for another job. Advancement to this grade is determined by your ability to excel in the job.

Your Starting Salary $43,139-$67,852 Per Annum can fall anywhere within this range, but entry-level employees typically are offered the minimum. If you have strong credentials, you can negotiate this point. If you are being considered for a hard-to-fill job or your qualifications are highly specialized or top-notch, consider asking for a "signing bonus," or ask the agency to pay off your student loan debt. Agencies have authority (but not necessarily the money) to do both. As an entry-level employee, don't be discouraged if you start out at the bottom of the pay grade; focus instead on doing a great job, achieving steady promotions, and working at something you love to do!

Career/Career Conditional - Appointment
This is a permanent position.
Multiple full-time permanent positions

There are multiple jobs available – that's great news!

Search Recommendation No. 2:

From the first screen, type in "Student Jobs." A number of student jobs will appear that may be of interest; however, not all of the student jobs will appear.

Go to the Basic Search (a top link)
Search for:

Keyword Search:	Student Jobs
Location Search:	Select All (or select your state)
Job Category Search:	Select All (or search for a job, but that will greatly narrow your results)
Salary Range:	Leave blank
Applicant Eligibility:	Click NO if you have not worked for the government before and have not had military experience or any of the choices above this selection
Sort:	By date
View Description:	Detailed
Results:	U.S.-Wide, 221 jobs that start with the job title of "Student" and are at the entry-level grades, GS 5-7

Student Jobs – Official Office of Personnel Management Site

www.studentjobs.gov

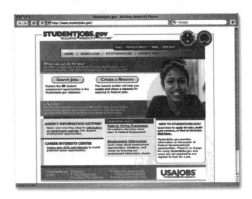

Sponsored jointly by OPM and the U.S. Department of Education, and the www.*studentjobs.gov* has information about nearly 300 different student employment opportunities. It also has a "career interest center" link that allows you to explore job opportunities based on your interests.

The e-scholar website, a subset of the studentjobs.gov site (*www.studentjobs.gov/e-scholar*) contains information about apprenticeships, internships, fellowships, scholarships, grants, and cooperative education opportunities available through federal agencies. This site will be useful to anyone from high school through post-doctoral educational students.

If you search for all jobs, all locations you can find student internships (STEP and SCEP programs as described in Step 2 and 3 of this book).

AvueCentral Recruiting System

www.avuecentral.com

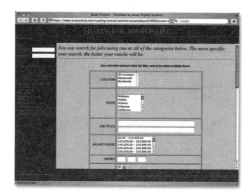

Avuecentral.com is a question-driven system developed and maintained by Avue Digital Services, a private industry company providing recruitment services for federal agencies. AvueCentral posts federal vacancy announcements, and receive and assess job applications for the federal government through their website (www.avuecentral.com) Agencies that use avuecentral.com place their job announcements here as well as on the OPM website (*www.usajobs.opm.gov*). Avuecentral.com is a free, easy-to-use website.

You can input your resume into their database with their resume builder and apply for jobs with any of their client agencies with a simple click. The search screen is simple to scroll through, with as many as 20 job announcements per screen.

> *NOTE:* You can find federal jobs on avuecentral.com, but only with agencies that are contracted with AvueCentral. If you want to apply for a job with an agency that does not use avuecentral.com, then you must go to USAJobs or to the agency's website to learn about the job and apply for it.

Announcements	Specific – good list of duties
Closing Dates	Current listings only
Resume Builder	10 screens, copy and paste
Job Duties Length	4,000 characters
Registration / Profile	Yes
Job-Specific Questions	Yes
Self-certify Your Skill Level	Yes
Essays / Examples	Possible
Multiple Choice	Yes
Yes / No Questions	Yes
How to apply	Go to announcements, answer questions
Track & Follow-up	HR staff name & phone on announcement

QuickHire
www.quickhire.com

QuickHire is another commercial company that developed a question-driven automated system for federal hiring. The company developed and maintains the system, but individual agencies actually apply it to meet their

needs. The agencies maintain their own applicant databases. Thus, while numerous agencies use QuickHire as their database and assessment tool, you must complete a separate registration form, and submit a separate resume to each user agency. And because agencies have control over how they use the system, the information in the vacancy announcements, and the information they require, depends upon the agencies themselves.

You can see a list of QuickHire's clients on their website (*www.quickhire.com*). QuickHire was recently purchased by Monster.com.

Announcements	Both descriptive and a few generic
Closing Dates	Current listings and a few open inventory
Resume Builder	One online field, copy and paste
Job Duties Length	16,000 characters – entire resume
Registration / Profile Questions	Yes
Supplemental Data Sheet	Yes
Job-Specific Questions	Yes
Self-certify Your Skill Level	Yes
Essays / Examples	Yes, at agency option
Multiple Choice	Yes
Yes / No Questions	Yes
How to Apply	Go to the announcement , answer questions, follow instructions
Fax or Mail	Requested information can be faxed or mailed
Track & Follow-up	HR staff name and phone on

The name, QuickHire, implies that a student can be hired quicker, but that's not necessarily true here. The system is efficient, but the timing will be similar to other automated hiring systems.

Department of Defense (Resumix™)

Department of Defense agencies (including the military services for their civilian hiring) use Resumix™, a resume-driven system. NASA also uses this system.

A key difference between this and the other automated hiring systems we have mentioned is that Resumix™ does not use your answers to job-specific questions to determine whether, and how well, you are qualified for a job. Like the other systems, it does have a group of personnel-type questions necessary to establish your account and to determine your eligibility for federal employment. After that, the focus is on the content of your resume.

Since all Department of Defense agencies use Resumix™, it is tempting to believe that one registration and one resume could be used for all civilian jobs having similar qualifications requirements across all of DoD, Army, Air Force, Navy, and the Marine Corps. Not so! While the system is commonly used, the requirements are specific to each user. So Army, Air Force, Navy (including the Marine Corps) and DOD all have unique requirements for their Resumix™ users. This is also true for NASA, which is not part of DoD.

To you, the job applicant, the obvious differences among the various DoD users are the length of the allowed resume, and whether they have provided a mechanism for easy tracking and follow-up. Among DoD agencies, the vacancy announcements may vary in the amount of detail they provide. Below we provide information about key websites to visit to apply for civilian jobs in the Department of Defense and the military. Remember, you can also find jobs in these departments on the USAJobs website, but you will be redirected to the specific departmental (e.g., Army, Navy) website to actually apply for a specific job.

The next four websites use Resumix Recruitment Systems: Navy, DCA, Army, and OSD.

Department of the Navy Civilian Jobs (Resumix)
www.donhr.navy.mil

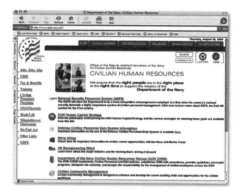

The U.S. Navy and Marine Corps have their own website on which you can post your resume. You may copy and paste your resume into their online resume builder, then search for announcements that match your qualifications. Go to the "Jobs, Jobs, Jobs" page to search for civilian job vacancies by geographic area, salary, or job title.

Internships with the Navy or Marines are also listed on this website. You MUST apply for jobs or internships through this system. The resume builder on this website is very simple and easy to complete.

NOTE: (Department of Navy) announcements are not particularly descriptive. They may have "generic" job descriptions instead of specific "duties," like other announcements. These are "Open Inventory" or database announcements.

Jobseekers may not take these employment opportunities seriously because the closing dates for the jobs can be 2012. However, they are real jobs; HR staff will search for the best candidates when a supervisor has a position to fill.

Agencies Served	U.S. Navy and U.S. Marines
Databases	8
Announcements	Generic – short descriptions of duties
Closing Dates	Current listings and Open Inventory
Resume Builder	8 Screens. Copy and paste
Job Duties Length	7,500 characters
Registration / Profile Questions	Yes
Supplemental Data Sheet	Yes
Job-Specific Questions	No
Self-certify Your Skill Level	No
Essays / Examples	No
Multiple Choice	No
Yes-No Questions	No
How to Apply	Self-Nominate after resume is in database
Track & Follow-up	Not easy, no automated system.

Defense Logistics Agency (Resumix)
www.dla.mil

The Defense Logistics Agency (DLA) is a U.S. Department of Defense (DoD) agency. It provides worldwide logistics support for the missions of the United

States military departments and the Unified Combatant Commands under conditions of peace and war. It also provides logistics support to other DoD components and certain federal agencies, foreign governments, international organizations, and others as authorized. DLA currently is engaged in a Business Systems Modernization project that will replace mission critical legacy systems with a new enterprise architecture based on Commercial Off the Shelf (COTS) software and best commercial practices.

NOTE: The DLA website is unique because it allows you to receive a list of your keywords and skills by email after you submit your electronic resume to the database. This is a very helpful feature!

Agencies Served

Defense Logistics Agency
Defense Contract Management Agency
Defense Contract Management Agency International
Defense Supply Systems
Defense Distribution Center
Defense Logistics Information Center
Defense Reutilization Marketing Center
Defense Human Resources Center

Announcements	Both descriptive and generic
Closing Date	Current listings and Open Inventory
Resume Builder	8 Screens Copy and paste
Job Duties Length	3,000 characters
Registration / Profile Questions	Yes
Supplemental Data Sheet	Yes
Job-Specific Questions	No
Self-certify Your Skill Level	No
Essays / Examples	No
Multiple Choice	No
Yes / No Questions	No
How to Apply	Self-Nominate after resume is in database
Track & Follow-up	HR staff name and phone on announcement

Department of the Army Civilian Personnel (Resumix)

www.cpol.army.mil

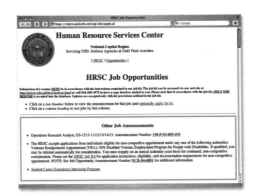

Although the U.S. Army posts its civilian vacancies on the USAJobs website, if you would like to be considered for a civilian position at any Army duty location, you MUST locate the vacancy announcements here and post your resume into the Army's resume builder. If you are interested in civilian positions with the U.S. Army, you might save time by going directly to this website to find the announcements and apply for the jobs.

Agencies Served	U.S. Army military bases and agencies
Announcements	Both descriptive and generic
Closing Dates	Current listings and Open Inventory
Resume Builder	8 Screens; copy and paste
Job Duties Length	3,000 characters
Registration / Profile Questions	Yes
Supplemental Data Sheet	Yes
Job-Specific Questions	No
Self-certify Your Skill Level	No
Essays / Examples	No
Multiple Choice	No
Yes / No Questions	No
How to Apply	Self-Nominate after resume is in database
Track & Follow-up	ANSWER system – track your job offers in a great database

Office of the Secretary of Defense, Pentagon (Resumix)

www.whs.pentagon.mil/persec.whs.mil/hrsc/empinfo.html

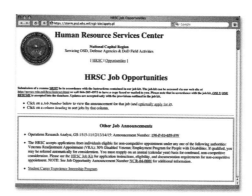

You can find specific jobs with closing dates on this website. There is a resume builder on this website also with its own database. You may submit your resume and select your job announcements.

Agencies Served	Office of the Secretary of Defense, Defense agencies, and DoD field activities
Announcements	Descriptive
Closing Dates	Current listings
Resume Builder	8 Screens; copy and paste
Job Duties Length	3,000 characters
Registration / Profile Questions	Yes
Supplemental Data Sheet	Yes
Job-Specific Questions	No
Self-certify Your Skill Level	No
Essays / Examples	No
Multiple Choice	No
Yes / No Questions	No
How to Apply	Self-Nominate after resume is in database
Track & Follow-up	HR staff name & phone on announcement

National Security Agency

www.nsa.gov

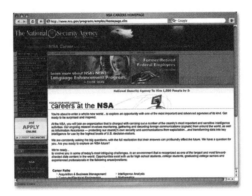

The National Security Agency is always hiring. Just submit your resume to their database and wait for a response. However, you cannot follow-upon your resume submission.

Agencies Served	National Security Agency
Announcements	Careers and jobs are both descriptive and generic
Closing Dates	Database collection
Resume Builder	12 screens. Copy and paste
Job Duties Length	3,000 characters
Registration / Profile Questions	Yes
Supplemental Data Sheet	No
Job-Specific Questions	No
Self-certify Your Skill Level	No
Essays / Examples	No
Multiple Choice	No
Yes / No Questions	No
How to Apply	Submit your resume and profile to database
	Check your target jobs on the shopping cart
Track & Follow-up	No system for applicant; wait for HR contact

Finding keywords and skills in the vacancy announcement

Once you have found a vacancy announcement, read it thoroughly, and determined that it's a job meant for you, the hard work begins! Analyzing a vacancy announcement for keywords is a crucial step in the federal job search process. By identifying keywords, you can customize your application materials to the announcement, which can improve your chances for being Best Qualified for the position and go to the next level, which would be the supervisor's review and possible interview.

> Why should a candidate use keywords in his, or her federal resume? So that either the automated system searching for skills or the human Federal HR specialist can quickly find the best candidates!

Carefully read both the "duties" and the "qualifications" sections in the announcement. Use a highlighter to mark the important skills and duties listed. Include these keywords (or most of them) as they pertain to your skills and qualifications gained from your courses, employment, or other experience. By meticulously adhering to this formula, your resume will clearly show that you meet the qualifications of the position, and your application package will stand out favorably. Look at the following announcement samples and the keywords that are in bold. These four announcements have a wide range of grade level and salary offerings, showing room for advancement. On-the-job training is expected and experience will be gained in the lower grades. It is possible to enter these positions at any of the grades listed based on your background and experience. Vacancy announcements with multiple grade offerings are your best option for career opportunities in government.

> Why is it important to be Best Qualified for a position? *Best Qualified* is the designation for those who will be forwarded to the supervisor. From the best qualified list, the supervisor will select the applicants he or she wants to interview.

Announcements with promotion potential and good keywords

EXAMPLE 1

U.S. Agency for International Development Agency

Position Title, Series, Grade: NEW **Entry Professional Program, Contracting** Officer, FS-4 Salary: $41,379.00 - $74,994.00 Annual
Duty Location(s): Worldwide

Contracting Officers in USAID **plan, negotiate, award, and administer contracts, grants, and other agreements** with individuals, firms, and institutions to carry out USAID financed projects. Duties include providing **technical guidance and assistance** to USAID's overseas and Washington staffs, and host country officials in the **negotiation and awarding of contracts and grants.**

Duties:
Supports activities within the contracting sector by **reviewing and analyzing data; developing strategies, analytical models, and methodologies; and providing assistance and advice on contracting issues.** Develops, oversees, manages, and evaluates contracting and assistance activities.

Designs, implements, monitors, and assesses programs that encompass a range of contracting and assistance activities such as procurement analysis, contract negotiation, contract cost/price analysis, and policy review. Plans, negotiates, awards, and administers **contracts**, grants, and other agreements with individuals, firms, and institutions to carry out USAID financed projects.

Plans and/or accomplishes special projects.

KNOWLEDGE, SKILLS AND ABILITIES:

Knowledge of **contracting laws, regulations, principles, policies, and procedures.**

Ability to **manage and build teams.**

Ability to **communicate effectively other than in writing.**

EXAMPLE 2

Drug Enforcement Agency

POSITION: Forensic Chemist, Gs-1320-5/7/9/11
SALARY RANGE: GS-5, $31,302 - $38,529; GS-7, $38,767 - $47,713; GS-9, $41,342
- $52,286; And GS-11, $47,078 - $60,317
FULL PERFORMANCE LEVEL: GS-12
VACANCY ANNOUNCEMENT NUMBER: 04-27
WHO MAY APPLY: All United States Citizens
TYPE OF APPOINTMENT: Permanent/full-time
OPENING DATE: 06-25
CLOSING DATE: 07-12
DUTY LOCATION(S): North Central Laboratory, Chicago, Illinois
NUMBER OF VACANCIES: 3 Or More Positions

DUTIES: Performs **chemical and physical tests** and **instrumental analyses** to detect
the presence of a **controlled substance** and determine its concentration in a **drug
sample. Establish the identity and concentration of accompanying adulterants**
and dilutents whenever possible. Render testimony as to his/her findings in Federal,
State, or local courts.

Advises and may assist in the performance of certain enforcement actitviies such
as clandestine laboratory seizures and vacuum sweeping searches for controlled
substances.

Operate analytical instrumentation such as IR, UV, and Fluorescence
Spectrophotometer, Gas Chromatograph, and GC/MS. Revise and develops
procedures as necessary to accomplish the analyses of more complex drug mixtures
or trace quantities of a particular substance.

Write a laboratory report, which describes all the tests performed, calculations, and
conclusions.

Testifies In Federal And State Courts As An Expert Witness; Presents
Technical Testimony In Laymen's Terms, **Defends Analytical Methods** And Results
Against Rigorous Cross Examination By Defense Attorneys. Assist Prosecuting
Attorneys In Preparation Of Technical Aspects Of Case.

QUALIFICATION REQUIREMENTS:
BASIC REQUIREMENTS:
GS-05: (A) Degree: Physical Sciences, Life Sciences, or Engineering that included 30
Semester Hours In Chemistry, Supplemented by course work In Mathematics
Through Differential and Integral Calculus, and at least 6 Semester Hours Of Physics.
Or (B) Combination Of Education And Experience - course Work Equivalent To A
Major As Shown In (A) Above, Including At Least 30 Semester Hours In Chemistry,
Supplemented By Mathematics Through Differential And Integral Calculus, And At Least
6 Semester Hours Of Physics, Plus Appropriate Experience Or Additional Education.

EXAMPLE 3

DEPARTMENT OF THE ARMY
Vacancy Announcement Number: WTEJ04951531

Opening Date: July 01, 20xx **Closing Date:** July 30, 20xx
Position: Electronics Engineer, GG-0855-5/07/09/11/12
Salary: $31,302 - $76,261 Annual
Place of Work: Assistant Secretary of the Army, Threat Simulation Management Office, Redstone Arsenal, AL - Duty Station: Fort Bliss, TX
Position Status: This is a permanent. --Full Time
Number of Vacancy: 1

Duties: Serves as an electronics engineer involved in the **intelligence design, development** and **lifecycle production** and **deployment of hardware threat systems** for the Army Threat Simulator Program with particular emphasis on **electronic subsystems.**

Assignments include several **air defense related areas such as early warning radars, fire control radars, ir systems, c3 systems, anti-aircraft artillery directors and jammer systems.**

Technology areas represented by these air defense categories include **radar transmitters, receivers, signal processing, moving target indicators, data display systems, mobile system design, packaging techniques, system life cycle engineering system test procedures and system instrumentation.**

QUALIFICATIONS:
· GS-05: 4 year course of study leading to a bachelor's degree directly related to this occupation.
· GS-07: Bachelor's degree directly related to this occupation and 1 year of experience directly related to this occupation equivalent to at least the next lower grade level, or 1 year of graduate level education, or superior academic achievement.
· GS-09: Bachelor's degree directly related to this occupation and 1 year of experience directly related to this occupation equivalent to at least the next lower grade level, or 2 years of progressively higher level graduate education leading to a master's degree or master's or equivalent graduate degree.
· GS-11: Bachelor's degree directly related to this occupation and 1 year of experience directly related to this occupation equivalent to the next lower grade level, or 3 years of progressively higher level graduate education leading to a ph.D. Degree or ph.D. Or equivalent doctoral degree.
· GS-12 and above: Bachelor's degree directly related to this occupation and 1 year of experience directly related to this occupation equivalent to the next lower grade level.
· The experience described in your resume will be evaluated as related to the qualifications, knowledge, skills and abilities required for this job.
· One year of experience in the same or similar work equivalent to at least the next lower grade or level requiring application of the knowledge, skills, and abilities of the position being filled.

EXAMPLE 4

DEPARTMENT OF COMMERCE,
NATIONAL INSTITUTE OF STANDARDS AND TECHNOLOGY

Opening Date: 01/20
Closing Date: 12/31

Position: **INFORMATION TECHNOLOGY SPECIALIST**
Zp-2210-05/15

Salary: $26,990 - $127,434 Per Year

THIS IS AN ONGOING RECRUITING FILE FOR POTENTIAL VACANCIES.
DUTY LOCATION: Gaithersburg, Md (from time to time, a small number of
Vacancies may be located at sites other than Gaithersburg, Md.)
WHO MAY APPLY: all qualified applicants

BASIC REQUIREMENTS
A. 4-Year course of study leading to a bachelor's degree; or
B. 3 Years of general experience, 1 year of which was equivalent to at least GS-
4. General experience is experience that provided a basic knowledge of data
processing functions and general management principles that enabled the applicant
to understand the stages required to automate a work process. Experience may
have been gained in work such as computer operator or assistant, computer
sales representative, program analyst, or other positions that required the use or
adaptation of computer programs and systems.

IN ADDITION TO THE ABOVE BASIC REQUIREMENTS, the following is required
to qualify at the pay bands indicated:
Pay band I (equivalent to GS-5): basic requirements only.
Pay band II (equivalent to GS-7/9):
   A. 1 Full year of graduate level education; or
   B. Being in the upper third of the graduating class in the college, university, or major
      subdivision; 3.0 Or higher out of a possible 4.0 Based upon 4 years of education, or as
      computed based on courses completed during the final 2 years of the curriculum; 3.5
      Or higher out of a possible 4.0 Based on the average of the required courses completed
      in the major field or the required courses in the major field completed during the final
      2 years of the curriculum; or c. One year of specialized experience equivalent to at
      least pay band i or GS-5. Some examples of specialized experience include: **translating
      detailed logical steps developed by others into language codes** that computers accept
      where this required understanding of procedures and limitations appropriate to use
      of a **programming language; interviewing subject-matter personnel** to get facts
      regarding work processes, and **synthesizing** the **resulting data** into charts showing
      information flow; operating PCS with various procedures responding to commands
      and unscheduled halts; scheduling the **sequence of programs** to be processed by
      computers where alternatives had to be weighed with a view to **production efficiency;**
      and preparing **documentation on cost/benefit studies** where this involved summarizing
      the material and **organizing** it in a logical fashion.

Pay band III (equivalent to GS-11/12):

A. Ph.D. Or equivalent doctoral degree; or

B. 3 Full years of progressively higher level graduate education leading to such a degree; or

C. One year of specialized experience equivalent to at least pay band II or GS-9. Specialized experience is defined as experience that demonstrated Accomplishment of **computer project assignments** that required a range of knowledge of computer requirements and techniques. For example, assignments would show, on the basis of **general design criteria** provided, experience in **developing modifications** to parts of a system that required significant **revisions in the logic or techniques used in the original development.**

Pay band IV (equivalent to GS-13/14):

One year of specialized experience equivalent to at least pay band III or GS-12.

Pay band V (equivalent to GS-15):

One year of specialized experience equivalent to at least pay band IV or GS-14.

ENTRANCE PAY RANGE: nist pay band information may be found at *www.nist.gov*

Conclusion

Searching for optimum internship and job vacancy announcements is challenging. Finding announcements for which you are qualified, analyzing those announcements for keywords, and using them in a relevant context in your resume is critical to the success of your federal job search campaign. Take your time and thoroughly examine the possibilities. That time will be well spent! The next step will give you tips on writing an effective federal resume so that you will be identified as a highly qualified candidate and gain an interview!

Q&A with Mariana Pardo, Team Leader at USAJobs

What is the best way to find student jobs on USAJobs?

The calls I often get are from parents who say, 'I'm looking for summer employment for my child, but can't find it.' And it's hard to find the announcements for them. Sometimes the word internship is not an effective way to search, so they should also try temporary jobs, temporary employment, student or summer.

Last week I met with a recent graduate who was looking for a job and I gave them the same recommendations as the ones you have in your book. Sometimes it's better to search for All on USAJobs. After the student gets a lot of results, then they can start to target and draw down that list. Initially, however it's important to see what's out there. You end up becoming a much more educated researcher.

We definitely encourage students to contact us with questions through the USAJobs website or by calling.

Q&A with Bryan Hochstein, Quickhire Government Solutions Monster.com

What changes can we expect to see on USAJobs in the future?

Application Integration is our new improvement at USAJobs and is scheduled to be released in early fall. Applicant integration will provide applicants the ability to sign on once at USAJobs and apply to any integrated solution, like QuickHire. Personal information will flow directly to the system where the applicant wishes to apply. This includes the applicant's selected resume, veteran's preference, etc.

Once this data is sent the applicant will use QuickHire as they would if they had signed on directly. This is going to really reduce the amount of time applicants register and apply on the different sites, while providing the flexibility demanded by our customers.

After Application Integration is complete, we will make updates to Application Status Integration, so that the status of every position applied for will be available on USAJOBS.

We're making great progress. Even before our acquisition, we made it very clear to OPM and our customers that we believe it's in everyone's best interest that the website succeeds. We fully support it, as do our customers.

WRITING YOUR FEDERAL AND ELECTRONIC RESUMES

Calvin Kline
A.A., Aviation Maintenance Technology
A&P Mechanic, Willing to join the U.S. Air Force Reserves

I didn't exactly appreciate the 3 R's in high school (reading, writing, 'rithmetic). My favorite courses were Welding, Machine Shop, Drafting, Automotive Drive Train, Heating/AC, and Diagnostics and Electrical. In my spare time, I purchased, repaired and sold custom-built automobiles, such as a 1977 Porsche 930 and a 1976 FJ40 Four Wheeler (rebuilt and restored from the frame up), and rebuilt and restored dirt bikes and collectibles. I was my sister's best friend when she needed her car fixed.

Anyway, I thought I might do well as an A&P Mechanic with an AAS in Aviation Maintenance Technology, and that getting a private pilot's license would be cool. Then my career ideas started to gel. I wanted new mechanical and technical challenges and I wanted to contribute to the safety and quality service for Defense and Homeland Security war fighting operations. I have decided to begin a federal civil service career as A&P Mechanic or Fixed Wing Mechanic. Later on, I may move into management or into specialized production planning or management positions in aircraft operations.

Read Calvin's resume on the CD-ROM.

How can I stand out against my competition?

Your federal resume <u>is</u> your federal application. This is the most important document you will write and submit for a Federal job. You may be required to submit other documents, but the resume is your primary application. Of all the steps in the book, this one is the most important. If you apply for jobs for which you are qualified, the resume serves as your first impression, and is what may make you stand out against your competition.

The typical length of a student or recent graduate federal resume is 2 to 3 pages! That's different from private industry. The federal student HR recruiters want to know more about you in writing to determine the Best Qualified candidates and consider you for an interview.

A common problem expressed by students regarding resume writing is that they feel they have nothing important to say. .. or they haven't worked enough … or they haven't worked at all.

Writing a professional resume is challenging for students, but not impossible! Our goal in this book is to help you present yourself as a young professional with potential, education, skills, interests, enthusiasm, talent, and the ability to learn, as well as contribute to a government agency or office.

This is a two-part chapter. The first part will focus on resume content; the second part will focus on the three resume formats you will need to apply - Paper, Flexible Electronic and Resume Builder Resumes.

What Federal Human Resources Staff and Supervisors are looking for

Before we discuss how to write an effective federal resume, let's review what HR professionals are looking for. Here is official information from the Office of Personnel Management on "What to include in your Resume." Some of this information is distinctively different from private industry resumes.

Federal Resume Requirements (from OPM's Form OF-510)

REQUIRED INFORMATION FOR RESUME*:

1. Announcement number, title, and grade of the position for which you are applying.
2. Your full name, mailing address, and day and evening telephone numbers.
3. Your e-mail address (please provide if available – failure to provide will not affect the processing of your application.)
4. Your Social Security number.
5. Country of citizenship.
6. High school attended which includes name of high school, location (city/state), and date of diploma or GED.
7. Work experience (Paid and non-paid experience related to the job for which you are applying. Include job title (YOU MUST INCLUDE SERIES AND GRADE IF FEDERAL JOB), duties and accomplishments, employer's name and address, supervisor's name and phone number, starting and ending dates (including month and year), salary, hours worked per week).
8. Indicate if your current supervisor may be contacted.
9. A list of other job-related training, skills (for example, languages, tools, machinery, typing speed, etc.), certificates and licenses, honor societies, awards, professional membership, publications, leadership activities, performance awards, etc.

*Please note that if your resume or application does not provide all the information requested in the vacancy announcement, you may lose consideration.

Federal Resume Writing Facts

A Federal resume is not the same as a private industry resume.
A Federal resume is not limited to one or two pages like private industry resumes. Federal HR reviewers prefer more information so that they may thoroughly evaluate you with regard to the position qualifications, knowledge, skills and abilities.

Do not assume anything-include it, and use keywords
Do not assume that the HR reviewer will understand that you have a certain skill if it's not clearly written in your resume. For example, if you state that you have spreadsheet design and development skills, but do not mention that you have skills in Excel or SPSS, they will not assume that you have Excel or SPSS skills. Or, if you indicate that you keyboard 60 wpm and have extensive computer skills and do NOT write that you have skill in Microsoft Word and Windows, they will not assume that you have skills in Word and Windows. State your skills clearly and concisely, and include everything that is important.

Add the details

Federal resumes and private industry resumes differ greatly in the amount of detailed information needed. For example, in private industry it is generally known what a Project Team Leader does. Therefore, a job description might could begin this way:

"Serve as Project Team Leader for (fill in the blank)."

For Federal HR staff, however, more detail is needed to describe the Project Team Leader responsibilities. Therefore, a federal resume job description might begin like this:

"Project Team Leader: Selected team members based on specific skill sets, delegated tasks, planned meetings, reviewed quality of team members contributions, set deadlines over 6 months, advised team members in strategies to complete their project duties, compiled and presented the final project. RESULTS: Completed a successful project on-time resulting in (fill in the blank)."

One resume fits all

We mentioned earlier in this book that "one well-written federal resume is all you need." Most of the online resume databases will allow you to submit only one resume at a time. That's why we recommend that you write one resume that covers the skills for your target positions – even if you have 2 or 3 target positions. You can change your resume, but the new resume will replace the original one and you never can tell when the HR recruiters will download the resumes for the announcements. To be safe, it's best to cover your skills in one resume when you are submitting online.

Once you have determined which of your skills and experiences are most relevant to your target positions, the information contained in one federal resume should be sufficient to respond to each application. The format may change depending on the resume builder and database, as you will see later in this chapter, but each format will be based on one basic resume. You may adapt the resume here and there with a few additional keywords based on the announcement language, but basically one resume will be useful for all applications. Are you ready to write? All right, let's go.

Federal Resume Sections

1. Name, Address, and Federal Job Profile Information – Distinctively Federal
2. Summary of Skills
3. Keywords and Core Competencies
4. Education
5. Work Experience and Internships
6. Other Information

1. Name, Address and Federal Job Profile Information – Distinctively Federal

The following items should be included in your Personal Information or Resume Builder Profile:

PERSONAL INFORMATION:

NAME
HOME ADDRESS
TELEPHONE NUMBERS (Home, Cell and Work)
E-mail ADDRESS
SOCIAL SECURITY NUMBER
CITIZENSHIP
PAST FEDERAL EXPERIENCE
SPECIAL HIRING PROGRAMS:
   – Persons with Disabilities
   – Outstanding Scholar
   – Military Spouse
VETERANS' PREFERENCE
CLEARANCE
LANGUAGES
OBJECTIVE: TITLE, SERIES AND GRADE OF JOB SOUGHT
ANNOUNCEMENT NUMBER

SOCIAL SECURITY NUMBER – The government manages applications by name and SSN. In private industry, this is a serious security concern, but in the government, you MUST include your SSN on each page of your federal application.

CITIZENSHIP – Most federal jobs require U.S. citizenship, but on occasion, you might see a vacancy announcement that states that they will accept applications from non-citizens.

PAST FEDERAL EXPERIENCE – If you worked for the government for a summer, or in a temporary position, that experience may help you qualify for the job you are seeking or may help obtain you a higher grade. Previous permanent federal employment could give you reinstatement eligibility, allowing you to be hired without competition. If you don't include information about your past federal employment, it can't be considered. List the title of your past government job, grade, agency and dates. If there is more than one, include them all.

SPECIAL HIRING PROGRAMS – The government offers hiring programs for special populations where your application will be handled differently than other candidates. Are you qualified for one of these programs?

> **PERSONS WITH DISABILITIES** – People with disabilities can be hired without a vacancy announcement if they know a supervisor who can use their skills and has the "slot" to hire an employee. (For a more thorough description, see the accompanying CD-ROM.)

> **OUTSTANDING SCHOLAR** (Described in Step 2) – For specific occupational series (the list is on the CD-ROM), an agency can hire more quickly if you have a 3.45 GPA overall for your undergraduate degree. You might also read a vacancy announcement that is recruiting Outstanding Scholar students specifically. In these cases OUTSTANDING SCHOLAR should be stated very clearly on your resume.

> **MILITARY SPOUSE** – If you are the spouse of a military service member who has returned from an overseas assignment, you can receive special consideration. This special hiring authority applies to individuals

who accompanied their spouses/parents to an overseas assignment (military or civilian, including nonappropriated funds jobs). If these individuals are hired overseas through "local hire" provisions (which are excepted service appointments or overseas limited appointments), when they return to the U.S. they may apply for federal jobs in the competitive service under merit promotion announcements. "The U.S." includes the 50 states plus Guam, Puerto Rico, and the U.S. Virgin Islands. Qualifying overseas employment does not include employment in U.S. possessions, such as Puerto Rico or Guam.

To be eligible, the individual must (1) have worked as a "local hire" overseas for at least 52 weeks (some time may be waived under certain conditions); (2) meet all regulatory requirements for the job (e.g., citizenship); and (3) returned to the U.S. within the preceding 3 years.

VETERANS' PREFERENCE – Certain veterans have hiring preference for federal jobs because of their service to our country. In addition, under certain circumstances the (a) spouses, (b) unmarried widows or widowers, or (c) mothers of certain categories of veterans are eligible for this hiring preference. Persons eligible for this preference get 5 points (disabled veterans get 10 points) added to their passing scores. Preference eligibles must be selected for a job over any equally or lower ranked person who lacks this eligibility. Not everyone who served in the armed forces qualifies as preference eligible. Eligibility is based on specific criteria, such as active duty during a war, service in a campaign or expedition for which a campaign badge has been authorized, or during certain specified time periods. IF you are a veteran, include your military service, dates of service and any special honors, and be prepared to furnish proof of your military service (e.g., your DD-214 Form) if you claim preference eligibility.

SECURITY CLEARANCE – If you have, or ever have had a clearance, state the type of clearance and the dates at the top of the resume.

LANGUAGES – If you speak, read or write any other languages, include this information at the top of your resume. Indicate your oral, reading, and writing language skill level using these terms: fair, moderate, fluent. If you're not at least "fair," don't claim skill in the language!

Andrea Fritchey
PO Box 0000
Evergreen, CO 80437

Home or Cell: (303) 111-1111   Work: (303) 222-2222
Email: acfritchey111@aol.com

Social Security No.:	000-00-0000
Citizenship:	United States
Federal Status:	Visitor Information Assistant, GS-1001-5, 05/20xx
to	12/20xx USDA USFS Clear Creek Ranger
District	
Veteran's Preference:	U.S. Army, 7/99 to 7/03, Honorable Discharged
Clearance:	N/A
Hiring Program:	OUTSTANDING SCHOLAR
Languages:	Spanish (Conversational, Moderate Speaking)
OBJECTIVE:	**Human Resources Specialist, 201-5/7, promotion potential GS-11. ANN. # R10-03-1327rel2**

2. Summary of Skills

Your Summary of Skills is a great introductory paragraph to introduce your most relevant skills for the position. There are two types of summaries:

- Summary of Skills – a list of skills, competencies and keywords. You can use bullets or dashes to set off the list.
- Profile – a summary of your background, including critical skills, important competencies, highlights from education, synopsis of work experience. Written in sentence/paragraph structure, it is usually used by more experienced applicants.

Editing the keywords for various announcements
The Summary/Profile section may be reviewed and changed slightly depending on the announcement language.

3. Keywords and Core Competencies make your Application Stand Out!

Every job and industry has its own specific language. Each federal resume needs to include the appropriate keywords. Federal HR professionals are inundated with recruitment duties and have hundreds of applications to process. If your application contains the best keywords drawn from the position announcement, you make their job easier! The way to stand out from other qualified applicants is by using the keywords and skills from the announcement.

SAMPLES – Look at Sample 2 and 3 on pages 119 and 121 at the end of this chapter. You will see Summary of Skill sections that include the most relevant skills for the position.

Where can you find the federal keywords?

As discussed in Step 5, keywords can be found in vacancy announcements in several locations: Duties, Qualifications, Knowledge, Skills & Abilities, Job Questions, and sometimes in other paragraphs. Read the entire announcement for keywords to include in your resume.

Most Federal vacancy announcements tend to be long and tedious. You may be tempted to just scan it. Read the entire announcement, however, for content and keywords to help you understand the job!

The following announcement is filled with keywords, skills, and duties that should be addressed in the applicant's federal resume. The keywords are in bold.

U.S. Agency for International Development Agency

Position Title, Series, Grade: NEW ENTRY PROFESSIONAL PROGRAM, Contracting

Officer, FS-4; Salary: $41,379.00 - $74,994.00 Annual; Duty Location(s): Worldwide

Contracting Officers in USAID **plan, negotiate, award, and administer contracts, grants, and other agreements** with individuals, firms, and institutions to carry out USAID financed projects. Duties include providing **technical guidance and assistance** to USAID's overseas and Washington staffs, and host country officials in the **negotiation and awarding of contracts and grants**.

DUTIES:

Supports activities within the **contracting** sector by **reviewing and analyzing data; developing strategies, analytical models, and methodologies; and providing assistance and advice on contracting issues**.

Develops, oversees, manages, and evaluates contracting and assistance activities. **Plans** contracting and assistance activities such as **procurement analysis, contract negotiation, contract cost/price analysis, and policy review. Plans, negotiates, awards, and administers contracts, grants,** and other agreements with individuals, firms, and institutions to carry out **USAID-financed projects**.

KNOWLEDGE, SKILLS AND ABILITIES:

Knowledge of **contracting laws**, regulations, principles, policies, and procedures.

Ability to **manage and build teams**.

Ability to **communicate effectively** other than in writing.

Ability to communicate in **writing**.

Relevant majors are **business administration, public administration, law, banking, international affairs, procurement and contracting or finance with an emphasis on commerce, trade, and materials management**.

Relevant experience is defined as professional contracting or procurement work.

Writing your Knowledge, Skills and Abilities (KSAs) narratives will be discussed in detail in Step 7

KEYWORDS EXAMPLE

The following Summary of Skills includes the keywords and skills which were in bold from the previous announcement. This will be at the top of your federal resume.

SUMMARY OF SKILLS:

Contract Management – MBA coursework concentrated in contract management, including Federal Acquisition Regulations.

Customer Service and Technical Guidance for Contractor Support – Member of team providing customer service and technical support throughout system training and upgrades.

Developing Contracting Strategies – Strategic planning courses and projects demonstrate my ability to be resourceful and creative in reaching, writing and planning organizational strategies for business development and growth.

Team Leadership – Team leader with experience in planning projects, timelines and objectives for six different teams engaged in major class projects during my college years. Skilled in delegating and reviewing project status and follow-up. Recognize the importance of communication to keep projects moving.

Writing Skill – . Efficient researcher skilled in writing coursework, papers and research projects.

Communication – Experienced in theater, speech and debate and in making presentations throughout college.

Include your Core Competencies and soft Skills

Aside from basic qualifications for the job, you need a number of personal qualities or "soft" skills to fully perform a job. These soft skills enable you to STAND OUT from other applicants when your resume hits the supervisor's desk. Core competencies are a step beyond skills. They are skills unique to you—some learned, some that you were born with—that bring together all your qualities.

For example, your resume might include a section called "Computer Skills," listing your experience in Microsoft Word and Excel. However, computer skills are part of a core competency that may be called "communication" or "problem-solving." As you identify your skills, ask yourself, "Is this skill part of a bigger core competency? How do I use this skill?" Am I using spreadsheet programs to create stunning bar graphs in order to communicate clearly in presentations? Or am I using spreadsheet programs to analyze data and calculate equations for research? Or both?

Core competencies begin to paint the big picture of YOU. You are not just an amalgamation of random skills—you are a person who possesses unique experiences and skills that, when viewed together, unveil your character, capabilities and potential. When you include core competencies in your KSAs and federal resume, your application will become more three-dimensional and help you rise above the competition. Our Tips for Translation will help you reframe your hard skills and match your core competencies to each job announcement:

Tips for Translation
- Look at the big picture
- Do some research
- Find patterns
- Think like management

Look at the big picture. Obviously, you didn't stack up a bunch of student loans or eat Ramen noodles for four years just to learn Calculus, or the History of Fashion, or whatever. The classes you took present a unique portrait of who you are—even if you took mostly required courses. What do you envision yourself doing? Communicating with people? Working with your hands? Negotiating sales? Chances are, you will find your core competencies somewhere between the knowledge you've gained in school and your dreams.

Do some research. Informational interviews are a great way to find out exactly what it takes to win and keep a federal job. Informational interviews are just what they sound like—an interview to get information. If you don't know anyone who does the job you want, try joining a federal employee association or an association in your field. Most associations publish lists of members and their positions. Ask someone for fifteen minutes and find out what they really do! Every job is more complicated than the job description and you need to know the inside scoop.

Find patterns. You may be one of those lucky people whose life path was perfectly clear from childhood. Maybe you wanted to be in business ever since you hired your little brother to sell Girl Scout cookies for you. If you're not yet ready to blaze some career trail, try to examine how you would like to spend your time. Many of your hobbies and classes may connect in ways you wouldn't expect. Here are some ideas:

Dan
- Captain of his intramural soccer team
- Studied business management, marketing and pottery (his girlfriend dared him!)
- Loves to read car magazines and helped his mom buy her new car
CORE COMPETENCIES: negotiation, able to handle diverse opinions, thrives in high-pressure situations, takes risks and follows through on projects

Tenesha
- Works part-time as an Administrative Assistant in a real estate office
- Studied philosophy, history and writing
- Regularly attends meetings of her neighborhood association
CORE COMPETENCIES: attentive listener, able to retain details and integrate into complex problems, able to follow directions and participate passively when necessary.

Think like management. Federal job hunting is a serious sport and you should know the opposition before walking onto the field. Who makes the hiring decision for your job? Imagine yourself looking at ten resumes with almost identical qualifications. What would make you choose one over another? Try to identify that indescribable quality that distinguishes a winning resume in your field—then try to describe it. There are some core competencies that would just not appear in an actual announcement. Here are a few examples of qualities your manager might be delighted to find (but not explicitly state):

- Demonstrated commitment (i.e. not going to quit after we train him/her)
- Passion for _____
- Energy in the face of a huge bureaucracy
- Patience with difficult coworkers/customers/boss
- Able to clean up big mistakes without complaint
- Agreeable, friendly, flexible
- Unafraid to ask questions or for help

Sample Vacancy Announcement

This vacancy announcement is for an intelligence job at the National Geospatial Intelligence Agency. It is an excellent example of an announcement which utilizes key skills and core competencies. The position would be available for someone with a Master's degree and it's notable because even though the position is very serious the announcement uses soft language like energetic and enthusiastic, which are words you could use in your resume.

> Skills: <u>Underlined</u>
> Core Competencies: **Boldface**

NATIONAL GEOSPATIAL-INTELLIGENCE AGENCY
Visit our home page at www.nga.mil.
Our Mission: NGA provides timely, relevant, and accurate Geospatial Intelligence in support of national security.
Our Vision: Know the Earth...Show the Way

VACANCY ANNOUNCEMENT
Announcement Number: 046651 Opening Date: July 6, 20xx
Closing Date: July 16, 20xx

POSITION TITLE & SERIES: Imagery Intelligence Analyst, NI-03 or 04
PAY BAND & SALARY RANGE: Band 03 $50,593 - $ 82,868
Band 04 $72,108 - $116,456
DUTY STATION: Washington, D.C.
AREA OF CONSIDERATION: External Applicants Only

ASSIGNMENT DESCRIPTION
Imagery Intelligence Analysts (IAs) exploit imagery from a number of sources and platforms in support of national security goals, concerns, and strategies. They primarily <u>analyze</u> military issues that include <u>force structure</u>, <u>capabilities</u> and <u>vulnerabilities</u> of potential adversaries, <u>weapons proliferation</u>, <u>emerging technologies</u>, and <u>treaty monitoring</u>. They may also work on diverse issues such as environmental concerns,

counternarcotics, disaster assessments, energy, infrastructure, industries, underground facilities, and economic issues. Briefing and writing skills are important. Foreign language skills are helpful but not essential.

ADDITIONAL INFORMATION PROVIDED BY SELECTING OFFICIAL: The Office of Counterproliferation (PC) is looking for **highly energetic, enthusiastic,** trained imagery analysts who with to work on the leading edge of emerging national security-related issues. PC has two positions available -- one in the Weapons of Mass Destruction Division's Biological and Chemical Weapons Branch (PCWW), and a second position in the Advanced Weapons Technology Division's Strategic Ballistic Missile Space Technology Branch (PCAX). PC supports a wide range of customers to include the President, NSC, DOD, State, Unified Commands, Service Intelligence Centers, and the rest of the Intelligence Community. We participate in a large number of International conferences and place a premium on providing ample training and travel opportunities for our analysts. Both divisions focus on providing analysis against the research, development, testing and production of facilities worldwide that are associated with a country's Weapons of Mass Destruction programs or against their Advanced Conventional Weapons Systems.

MANDATORY QUALIFICATIONS
Skills
Technical/Specialized Reading (IA); Imagery-Based Intelligence Writing; Intelligence Briefing; Predictive Intelligence Judgements; Imagery Analysis Professional Representation; Customer Service (IA); Quality Assurance (IA); Imagery Analysis (IA); Leadership Knowledges; Image interpretation principles; Intelligence analysis tradecraft

DESIRABLE QUALIFICATIONS
Skills
Data & Statistical Analysis; Collection Planning/Monitoring; Product Improvement; Product and Tasking Coordination; Softcopy Product Dissemination; Image Interpretation; Map Reading and Plotting; Mensuration; Database Management (IA); Analytical Innovation & Shortfall Identification; Intelligence Conclusion Formulation; **Self-Development; Personal Time Management; Mentoring (IA) Knowledges**

4. Education

Since you are just completing your education, this section is CRITICAL to consideration for a federal job or internship program. Your courses, projects, research papers and activities are likely to be what will impress the Human Resources staff and the hiring manager. If you don't have a degree yet, list the number of credit hours you have completed and whether they are semester or quarter hours.

You will primarily be using your education and academic experiences to become Best Qualified for your target position, so you will need to expand this information. You should list the education section before work experience.

Relevant Courses and Descriptions. The vacancy announcement will list any courses that are required for the position. Be sure to list the Relevant Courses in your resume in addition to providing a copy of your transcript. The course description can be important for critical courses so that the HR staff will see the keywords, and the supervisor will understand courses that may not be clear without the description.

Academic Projects. Many courses include a project or research paper where you work individually or as part of a team. Write about your major projects and papers. The HR reviewers will see keywords and skills that relate to the position. Since you are a recent or soon-to-be graduate, your most important experiences could be course projects and papers.

Academic Honors. This section may include scholarships, fellowships, the Dean's list, graduation with honors, honorary societies, letters of recognition, ROTC military honors.

Academic Activities. Your academic activities demonstrate specialized interests, skills, and values. If you are a member of a sports team, you demonstrate discipline, teamwork, ability to manage a schedule, and dedication. If you are in theater or debate, you demonstrate communications skills, practice, teamwork, and again, dedication to a group effort (which will be important in your federal career). Federal jobs are performed in teams many times—groups of employees combine to implement programs and provide services to various customers. Activities also show that you can handle multiple projects, deadlines and work with diverse groups.

Academic Papers and Publications. Writing articles, papers, presentations, speeches, and reports for courses, newspapers, and other print media can be greatly helpful when you are writing your KSA, "Ability to Communicate in Writing." Federal employees communicate in writing every day – via emails, briefings, researching and summarizing information, website content, memos, letters, and more. Writing is a critical skill in government, so include your writing experience from college.

Presentations. Depending on your major and degree, you may have had the opportunity to give presentations, speeches, and briefings. Make it clear in your resume that you have given presentations for courses, associations, or volunteer activities. "Ability to communicate other than in writing" is an important government skill. Federal employees talk and listen to customers, co-workers, other agencies, and contractors. You may negotiate, lead, or give briefings, using experience you gained in college.

Training, Workshops, Conferences. Be sure to include special workshops, training programs, and conferences you may have attended during college. Specialized courses demonstrate that you have sought out additional training and networked within a particular field of work.

Certifications. Separate your certification programs from your courses and internships. If you are certified in First Aid, Lifeguard Training, CPR, SCUBA, computers, or other certifications, include these. Job-related certifications are impressive to HR staffing specialists, as well as the manager.

5. Work and Internship Experience

This is either the most, or second most important section in your federal resume. That depends on your experience. Your paid and non-paid experience gained from jobs and internships is critical to how competitive your application is. One of the biggest challenges of writing your position descriptions is writing in some detail, including specific projects, knowledge gained, skills developed, and missions or programs supported.

This section of the federal resume is different from a resume aimed at private industry. A federal resume should include sufficient information so that HR reviewers can check your references, and determine how much time you spent performing specialized work during your work and internship experiences. Federal agencies may total up your hours spent doing a particular kind of specialized work to see if it amounts to a year or more. The agency then determines the level of the work experience. It is possible to qualify for a higher grade than you initially expected because of part-time work and internship experiences. But you have to furnish the information if you want it considered. Include the following information for each position that is relevant to your career objective:

Job Title
Workplace Name, Address, Zip Code
Ending Salary
Hours Per Week
Supervisor Name And Phone Number
Permission To Contact (Yes/no)

What if your supervisor is no longer there? What if the business closed, moved or changed names? Answer: Just write the supervisor's name and give a telephone number that will be answered (if possible). Or write this: Company is no longer in existence.

You can list your internships in the same section as your work experiences, or you can separate them so that they are clearly defined. Your internships provide knowledge in a certain field of work, skills and projects that could demonstrate qualifications. Internships could be paid or unpaid. Either way, you can acquire credit that may qualify you at a higher grade level. Be sure to add hours per week so that you can get credit for this experience.

Keys for Accomplishment Record

Your Accomplishments should demonstrate your competencies, NOT state your theoretical beliefs or philosophies. If we are asking them to write about their leadership skills, it is best if they tell us SPECIFICALLY what it is that they've actually done rather than their leadership philosophy, such as 'I take a contingency approach.' We're asking applicants to demonstrate for us very clearly and succinctly—in a few paragraphs—what they've done and what the results were. We are looking for results!
James Wilson, PMF Program

Work and School Projects and Accomplishments

If your positions or internships have been project based, then you should describe each project. Expressing achievement in the workplace is an excellent way to stand out from the competition.

Project lists. Keep notes on your projects, so that you may record your accomplishments not only for your resume, but for your KSAs and interview as well.

Track the following:
- Title of project/program
- Mission or objective
- Your role
- People with whom you communicated
- Major challenges or problems
- Results (products including reports, cost savings, improved efficiency, or service, etc.).

Accomplishments in job descriptions and Major Accomplishment sections.
Even if your job does not involve special projects, you should highlight accomplishments. Do this by literally listing selected accomplishments at the end of a job description set off by a sub-heading. If you have achieved

something special, large, or important in your career or life that you want to emphasize, you can create a "Major Accomplishments" section after the relevant jobs.

Include Recognition:
- Team reviews
- Professor reviews
- Articles from newspapers
- Awards
- Letters of recognition

Frequently Asked Questions:

In what order should jobs be listed?
Use reverse chronological order, listing your most recent position or project first, and work backward. However, if you have an older position or project that is more relevant to the vacancy than your most recent listing, list the older one first in order to highlight this relevant experience. Then title that section "Relevant Experience". If you are returning to government after having left, list your government experience first.

How far back should I go?
The most relevant positions are those within the last five or ten years.

I'm changing directions, so how do I handle courses and experience that really isn't relevant?
Those changing majors often have two types of courses and projects, with one type more relevant to an announced vacancy than the other. In this case divide the experience into separate sections with appropriate headings. You may want to de-emphasize the less relevant experience, even if it represents the majority of your history.

6. Other Information

Other information includes community service, special interests or hobbies, or information about skills and accomplishments that doesn't fit elsewhere else. Contrary to popular belief, such listings are not "fluff" and if done properly, and can even be an asset. HR personnel reading your resume may remember you specifically because of your outside interests. In practical terms, other information probably has the least direct relevance to the job you're applying for, so this section should be placed last on a federal resume. However, such placement does have the advantage of being the last thing a reader may see, and perhaps has the potential to create an impact.

Now that you have learned about content of a federal resume, Section Two is all about helping you format your resume for successful submission into an online resume builder or single online field, as an attached file, or by fax or regular mail. Again, since the "How to Apply" instructions vary, the format of your resume will also vary. We recommend three resume formats for students, depending on the application instructions.

Three Resume Formats for Student Federal Applicants

We have just demonstrated that the content is more detailed for federal than for private industry resumes. In this formatting section, we'll show three formats that can be used for your federal resume. Again, it is one basic resume, but formatted differently, depending on the agency's submission requirements and announcement instructions.

NOTE: The three samples shown here are also on the CD-ROM, and are actually longer than the two pages shown in this chapter.

1. RESUME BUILDER ELECTRONIC RESUME

Department of Defense agencies and NASA are using Resumix™, at least twelve agencies are using AvueCentral, many agencies are using USAJobs, and other agencies their own resume builders to collect resume information into their databases. These resume builders involve multiple fields where you can copy and paste text from your word processing file, or simply type in your information. **Suggestion for students:** Sample 1 demonstrates that you can use Job Blocks 1, 2, and 3 to write your education information. You can expand your course description, project descriptions, team projects, and skills.

Do not use any formatting for either of the electronic resumes. This means no bold, italics, or underlining; do not use bullets or indent text. Keep the text flush left and use paragraphing and ALL CAPS for highlighting important skills and information.

2. FLEXIBLE ELECTRONIC RESUME

The QuickHire system that many agencies use is very applicant friendly. You can copy and paste your entire resume into one field in about five seconds! Another feature is that you can organize your resume content any way that you choose. **Suggestion for students:** As you will see in Example 2, you can put your education first, then certifications and end with your work experience. You can even include a short cover letter in addition to the resume if you have enough space. The QuickHire resume field allows for 16,000 characters. That would be equal to five pages of text! Lots of room!

3. PAPER FEDERAL RESUME WITH FORMATTING FOR MANAGERS AND INTERVIEWS

Some announcements will ask you to mail your application, which will require a formatted resume. Or hopefully, you will land an interview – maybe in person. The supervisor will receive a copy of your electronic resume which will have no bold type, no indentations or formatting features to help them read the resume. If you are meeting the supervisor in person, you will need to take a formatted paper resume to the interview.

EXAMPLE 1

Example 1: Resume Builder Electronic Resume

SCOTT HAMPSTEAD
5555 University Blvd.
Hyattsville, MD 20783
Phone: (301) 333-3333
Email: scotth20202E@earthlink.net

OBJECTIVE
GS-0830-7 Federal Career Internship, Mechanical Engineer
U.S. Army Corps of Engineers, Baltimore, MD

JOB 1
B.S. IN MECHANICAL ENGINEERING HONORS PROGRAM
University of Maryland, College Park, MD, Expected July, 20xx
Overall GPA: 3.6/4.0; Engineering GPA: 3.7/4.0
(Qualifies for appointment at the GS-7 by meeting the criteria for Superior
Academic Achievement.)

Honors and Activities
NATIONAL MERIT SCHOLAR, MARYLAND DISTINGUISHED SCHOLAR
A.P scholar with honors, Dean's List (four times)
Maryland club lacrosse and intramural soccer (19xx-20xx)

Related Coursework
Calculus, Physics, Chemistry, Differential Equations, Statistics, Dynamics,
Thermodynamics, Introduction To Matlab, Fluid Mechanics, Electronics and
Instrumentation, Engineering Materials and Manufacturing Processes, Statistical
Methods of Product Development, Transfer Processes, Automotive Design,
Manufacturing Automation, Technical Writing, Human Resource Management,
Introduction to Transportation in Supply Chain Management.

Computer Skills
Word, Excel, PowerPoint, Pro-Engineer, Matlab.

JOB 2
TEAM LEADER AND TEAM MEMBER, University of Maryland College Park, 19xx
to present

Team Semester Projects:
REDESIGN OF THE DEWALT TRADESMAN DRILL using the nine-step product
development process. Directed the testing and building of a prototype
cordless/corded drill. Compared results to necessary specifications to determine
effectiveness of the design. Gave PowerPoint presentations on project results.
Utilized analytical tools such as the House of Quality, Weighted Decision Matrix,
Morphological Chart, and Functional Decomposition to redesign drill. 20xx
Design of Hybrid SUV for Future Truck competition. In charge of testing of the
performance of the electric motor. Analyzed complex schematics to determine
connector specifications and location. Negotiated the donation of connectors for
the high-voltage system. Researched torque curves for the stock engine and the
replacement engine. 20xx-20xx

EXAMPLE 1

JOB 3
TEAM PROJECT SKILLS, University of Maryland, College Park, MD
As Team Leader for more than 10 significant projects, developed skill in analyzing projects, delegating tasks and establishing timelines. Also developed the following engineering and project management skills:

- Draft project details
- Devise and recommend alternative methods of standardized analysis as a basis for solving problems
- Recommend and devise deviations to details
- Assist in reviews of engineering changes
- Review compliance to contract during design, development and production
- Evaluate control of baseline products
- Manage and/or witness tests
- Evaluate quality assurance activities
- Conduct cost and schedule analysis and estimations
- Manage engineering data collection and analysis

JOB 4
Sales Clerk, Village Antiques, 1000 Old Frederick Road, Oella, MD 90909 (19xx-19xx) Supervisor: John Jones (410) 444-4444; 18 hours/wk. salary: $12 per hour
Responsible for customer service, sales, daily operation of store

EDUCATION:
B.S. IN MECHANICAL ENGINEERING HONORS PROGRAM
University of Maryland, College Park, MD
Centennial High School, Ellicott City, MD, Class of 1999

AWARDS AND RECOGNITIONS:
College GPA: July, 2003; Overall GPA: 3.6/4.0; Engineering GPA: 3.7/4.0
High School Academic Honors: Honor Roll; Cumulative GPA: 3.6 / 4.0; National Merit Finalist/Scholar; A.P Scholar with Honor
High School Significant Courses:
Gifted and Talented English, Social Studies; Math and Science course work
A.P. Psychology, A.P. Statistics; A.P. English 12, A.P. Calculus One and Two

EXAMPLE 2

Example 2: Flexible Electronic Resume

Copy and paste your resume into one online field! Resume format and sections can be flexible to feature the Summary of Skills and Education or Experience. This sample lists education first, but experience is also important.

LISA E. REDDEN
SSN: 222-22-2222
Cell: 703-444-4444
Home: 703-333-3333
10366 Smith Lane
Manassas, VA 20110
Redden77@aol.com

U. S. Citizen: Yes
Veterans Preference: No
Federal Civilian Status: Student Temporary Employment Program (STEP), 12/20xx-05/20xx, and 07/20xx-08/20xx.
Highest Civilian Series and Grade Held: GS-303-2

OBJECTIVE
Public Affairs Specialist, GS-1035-5/7, Announcement 30303, U.S. Dept. of Agriculture, Food Safety & Inspection Service

SUMMARY OF SKILLS
Self-reliant and focused in academic and professional pursuits.
Outstanding skills in written and oral communications.
Team player; identify needs and fill them.
Energetic and willing to handle multiple projects
Writing, editing and publication assistant
Research, analysis and information gathering
Able to multi-task and prioritize projects; effective under pressure
Computer proficiencies: MS Office Professional (Word, Excel, Access, PowerPoint, and
    Outlook), PhotoShop, ScheduALL, Citrix, Internet, and E-mail.
Office equipment: phones (teleconferencing) and FedEx labelers.
60 words per minute keyboard.

EDUCATION

GEORGE MASON UNIVERSITY (GMU), Fairfax, Virginia 22032.
B.S. IN MASS COMMUNICATIONS AND JOURNALISM, Expect to graduate May 20xx.

Relevant Journalism Courses:

NEWS REPORTING AND WRITING
Basic news gathering, journalistic writing. Developing story ideas. Problems associated with handling of news/features. Professional standards/responsibilities.

VISUAL JOURNALISM
Introduction to nonfiction storytelling in multiple visual media. Photojournalism,

news videography, print/Web graphics. Conceptualizing stories, information gathering, camera work, editing, presentation strategies for print/electronic media.

PUBLIC AFFAIRS REPORTING
Reporting news of public institutions, including municipal, county, state, and federal administrative/legislative agencies and the courts. Politics and public companies.

PUBLICATIONS EDITING
Improving news/information copy through stylistically correct copyediting/ rewriting. Selection/editing of news-editorial content for newspapers, magazines, and online services. Hands-on experience using news judgment to present information in print and on the Web.

OSBOURN PARK HIGH SCHOOL, Manassas, VA 20111. Advanced Diploma, 06/0xx. Graduated in the top third of the class.

HONORS and AWARDS
-Cash Award of $100 for superior performance during summer internship, 20xx
-Art AP Test score of 4 out of 5: awarded 4 semester hours credit at GMU.
-Member of the National Art Honors Society, 20xx-20xx
-Won Fire Safety Poster Contest for Camden County NJ, (First Place) and went on
   to State competition, 20xx.

TRAINING AND CERTIFICATIONS
Nextec Inc., Herndon, VA.
Completed A+ and Net+ Certification courses. Fall 20xx.

WORK EXPERIENCE
05/20xx to present, 40 hrs/wk, $15.32/hr, **INFORMATION SPECIALIST II**, Vistronix, Inc., McLean, VA. Supervisor, Sandra Arzabe, 1-800-659-7379 (may contact). Contract to 08/20xx.

PROGRAM ASSISTANT - COPS MORE (Making Officer Redeployment Effective). Maintained a time and attendance database for law enforcement officers on community policing projects on grants from the Dept. of Justice.

DATA ANALYSIS - CIVILIAN SURVEYS: Evaluated grantees' calculations on community policing projects for a rotational police staff of 100. Analyzed savings for hiring civilian personnel vs. utilizing sworn officers who would ordinarily be performing police duties.

10/20xx to 02/20xx, 20 hrs/wk, $10.50/hr, **RECEPTIONIST / ADMINISTRATIVE ASSISTANT**, Manpower Temporaries, Manassas, VA. For Cubic Transportation Systems, Chantilly, VA.

ADMINISTRATIVE SUPPORT: Provided engineering and business development support. Processed employee timecards, and maintain accurate records. Made travel arrangements for engineers. Finalized travel expense reports for Accounting. Maintained inventory of office supplies; prepared monthly order.

EXAMPLE 3

Example 3: PAPER FEDERAL RESUME

ERICKSON S. YATES
625 16th St., N.E. #7,
Washington, D.C. 20017
E-mail: EricksonYates@hotmail.com

Social Security No.: 000-00-0000
Citizenship: United States

Citizenship: United States
Federal Civilian Status: N/A

OBJECTIVE:
Writer-Editor, U.S. Department of State, Office of Publications

SUMMARY OF RELEVANT SKILLS:

- *Research*: Legislative, newspaper, Internet, Lexis/Nexis, International, Library of Congress, original research through email /Internet writing.
- *Writing*: Reports, correspondence, emails, PowerPoint copy, web content, newspaper articles, newsletter content.
- *Communicating in Writing*: Proficient in and enjoy researching, writing and editing all forms of reports, correspondence, and communications.
- *Project Coordination*: compiling information, planning and coordinating the completion of projects; tracking status, and managing details.
- *Liaison and Scheduling*: organized and efficient in scheduling and following-up on details and meetings.
- *Languages*: American Sign Language and Costa Rica Sign Language; Writing in English and fluent Spanish.
- *Computer Skills*: Microsoft Suite: MS Word, PowerPoint, Excel, Keyboard 50 wpm
- *Resourceful and Creative*: Able to complete projects, research information and meet deadlines through hard work and resourcefulness.

EDUCATION:

Gallaudet University, Washington, D.C., May 2003
Bachelor of Arts, Government and Spanish
GPA: 3.348. Semester hours: 138.

Honors & Awards:
Phi Sigma Iota Award (Foreign Language Honor Society).
Athletics Volunteer Award, Admissions/Concession Staff.
Dean's List, Gallaudet University, Spring 20xx. Fall 20xx, and Spring 20xx.
Theatre Carpenter Award, Gallaudet University Theatre Arts Department.

Represented Gallaudet College at the Department of State's "Disability Mentor's Day". Met Secretary of State Colin Powell. Was photographed with Mr. Powell and quoted in State Magazine, December 20xx, p. 19, *http://www.state.gov/documents/organization/27053.pdf*

<u>Research Paper Topics</u>
    History of Republic of Costa Rica
    Eisenhower—Desegregating Schools and the Supreme Court
    Hispanic Immigrations in United States
    Antonio Magarotto and World Federation of the Deaf

Georgia School for the Deaf, Cave Spring, Georgia, Diploma, May 1998

INTERNSHIPS – LEGISLATIVE AND ASSOCIATION

Student Intern, Costa Rica National Association of the Deaf
Asociación Nacional de Sordos de Costa Rica (ANASCOR), San Jose, Costa Rica
    Assisted the President and Board members by researching newspaper
    articles related to deaf community and ANASCOR, events and special
    projects. Supervisor: Jose Rene; (202) 444-4444; Yes, you may contact;
    Salary: $10/hour; 25 hours per week; Sept. – Dec. 20xx

Staff Assistant, U.S. Senator Max Cleland, United States Senate, Wash., D.C.
    Participated in the legislative process, including research on legislative
    issues, feeding information into database and drafting correspondence to
    Georgia constituents. Supervisor: Tiffany Edwards; (202) 444-4445; Salary:
    $8/hour; 20 hours per week; Summers 20xx, 200xx

ADMINISTRATIVE EXPERIENCE – THREE YEARS:
Postal Aide, Gallaudet Post Office, Gallaudet University, Washington, D.C.,
Student Assistant, the Office of the Provost, Gallaudet University, Wash., D.C.,
Lab Assistant, Government and History Department Computer Lab
Gallaudet University, Washington, D.C.

Conclusion

Developing the content of your federal resume is your most important task in applying for a federal job. To help you stand out, build the content through analyzing keywords, research appropriate announcements, include your best core competencies, and make sure that you use the correct application format, following the announcement instructions.

We're almost finished with the research and writing! One more writing step, then it's time to apply for federal jobs!

WRITE KSAS AND COVER LETTERS

Lauren T. Dobbin
Ph.D., Chemistry
Forensic Chemist, Federal Bureau of Investigation

Ever since my junior year in high school, I knew that I would pursue a career in the sciences, I was particularly interested in chemistry. In my sophomore year in college, I was offered an opportunity to take part in an independent research project under the direction of the chair of the department, Dr. Serge Schreiner. For three years, I worked year-round on the synthesis, characterization, and reactivity of new platinum complexes to be used as catalysts in the removal of sulfur from fossil fuels in an attempt to control the environmental problem of acid rain.

I was able to present my work at numerous American Chemical Society Meetings at the local, regional, and national level. It was during this time that I grew as a confident and independent scientist and I knew I wanted to make a difference in society with all of the chemistry I was learning. Dr. Schreiner truly served as an inspiration to me. He was always presenting me with opportunities to enhance my education and knowledge of chemistry and introduced me to the field of forensic chemistry.

I began researching agencies that offered positions in the field of forensic chemistry such as the FBI, ATF, and DEA. I initially started close to home and discovered that my parents were friends with someone who worked in the FBI Laboratory in Quantico, VA. That one contact soon led me to several others and the more I learned, the more I knew I wanted to work for the FBI.

Read Lauren's entire story and resume on the CD-ROM.

What is a KSA?

KSA is an acronym for "Knowledge, Skills, and Abilities." Federal agencies often assess job applicants by referring to KSAs, narrative statements written by the applicant that reflect successful performance in their background. When required, you will prepare written statements demonstrating how your training and experience equipped you with the Knowledge, Skills, and Abilities to do your job. In general, KSA responses are a key component to your application package as the agency develops the "short list" of candidates who are sent to the selecting manager. Federal internship announcements usually do not require KSAs, but you most likely will have to write KSA narratives if applying for jobs through standard vacancy announcements.

KSAs are referred to in several ways:
- Essays
- Examples
- Key Elements
- Narrative Statements*
- Narratives
- Placement Factors
- Quality Ranking Factors
- Statements of Qualifications
- Supplemental Statements

*There's a second type of Narrative Statement, see cover letters.

KSA Writing Tips:
- Most KSAs are 2/3 to 1 page in length; do not exceed 1 page per answer
- Put each KSA on its own page
- Include the question at the top of the page (correct any grammatical errors)
- Include 1-3, preferably 2, unique examples per KSA
- Use the CARC format whenever possible (Context, Action, Results, Challenge)
- Include keywords from the question and announcement
- Write in the first person; emphasize your personal contributions even when using a team activity as an example, "I did this…"

- Be sure your Federal resume supports all statements made in KSAs
- Spell out all acronyms
- Don't pad your answer, but never leave a KSA blank
- Put your name and SSN number on the top of each page of your KSAs.

KSAs are designed to solicit detailed information about your training and experience to aid HR professionals in making qualitative distinctions among eligible applicants. They are used to "weed out" the less qualified applicants, and to move the better qualified ones closer to the interview stage. Completing KSA statements also prepares you for an interview. When combined with the "duties and responsibilities" portion of the vacancy announcement, writing KSAs better prepares you for job-related questions that the Federal manager may ask.

There is no mandated limit on the number of KSAs that an agency can request for an announcement, but a practical limit would be around seven. The number is likely to be greater as the grade of the vacancy (measuring duties and responsibilities) increases. For jobs at the GS-5, 7, or 9 level, three to five KSAs is typical.

KSA topics vary according to the requirements of the position. "Communication" is an important skill for most jobs; therefore, KSAs involving communication are common. Here are some examples of communication KSAs, ranging from simple to complex:
- Skill in oral communications.
- Skill in written communications.
- Skill in written and oral communications.
- Demonstrated ability to communicate technical results in a variety of formats (including oral presentations and publications) for both technical and non-technical audiences.
- Ability to communicate complex information effectively, orally and in writing as evidenced by: a) experience with a wide array of reporting formats and instructional activities presented to both scientific and non-technical audiences; and b) ability to create a collaborative work environment in order to facilitate constructive teamwork among participants with different, and sometimes hostile, perspectives.

The preceding five KSAs are complex for both you as an applicant as well as the Human Resources staff, who are required to rate or grade your answers. Be very clear with what you write so that they understand your answer for each element of the KSA.

Job-specific knowledge is another common KSA topic. Here's a sample:
- Basic knowledge of concepts, principles, and practices in the electrical engineering field.
- Professional knowledge of and skill in applying accounting concepts, principles, and methods.
- Knowledge of laws, regulations and procedures governing employment (staffing, pay, and employee benefits).
- Knowledge of health care systems and the role of Medicare, Medicaid, and other CMS programs in providing health care services to the nation's beneficiaries.
- Knowledge of major statistical computer packages and languages, including SAS, to be used to produce final results from data using appropriate statistical theory.

Writing your Accomplishments in KSAs and in your Federal Resume

You need to describe the context of your experience, what actions you took, and what results came from those actions. Be succinct and concise, and don't be modest. We're brought up to think about the team, 'We did this and We did that…,' because no one wants to seem like a maverick. But in this case, they're looking for the 'I.'

We know you were a part of a team. We know you didn't reduce the deficit by yourself! But if you've been a significant component of that team, you want to say so. You might say, 'I put the team together' or 'I worked behind the scenes to do this…' That's what we want to see. The more you can show us how you have distinguished yourself in the demonstrated areas about which we've asked helps a lot.
James Wilson, PMF Program.

How to Answer KSAs

Here's a tip on how to better understand a KSA subject. Use your imagination to re-think the KSA as a question, as if you were being interviewed (for draft purposes only).

> *KSA Example 1:*
> **1. Basic knowledge of concepts, principles, and practices in the electrical engineering field.**
> Think: Can you give me 2 or 3 examples of how you utilized your basic knowledge of the concepts, principles, and practices in the field of electrical engineering?

> *KSA Example 2:*
> **2. Skill in written and oral communications.**
> Think: Can you describe 2 or 3 examples of how you demonstrated your skills in written and oral communications?

Notice the rephrased statements include action verbs like "demonstrate" and "utilize." Even when the KSA does not include an action verb, you can assume the agency wants one or more examples of how you applied your knowledge, skills, and abilities in your background experiences.

An interview is your chance to make your resume come to life. KSAs offer the same opportunity. If an interviewer says, "Tell me about a time when you demonstrated your skills in written communications" you would probably not want to respond simply by saying, "Well, I have a bachelor's degree in English."

KSAs should focus on illustrative examples and always be as specific as possible. This includes using keywords from the question itself in your answer. You should also try to work in key words from the announcement. For example, if the job announcement says they are looking for someone "self-motivated," but "self-motivation" is not specifically in the KSAs, you should try to mention it somewhere-if it is one of your strengths.

On the other hand, be careful not to waste space elaborating on things not asked in the question. Let's say one KSA addresses written communications skills. (Remember, you are thinking, "Can you give me 2 or 3 examples

of how you demonstrated your skills in written communications.") That question should never be answered by waxing eloquently about the time you made a brilliant oral presentation in your World Lit class. Oral communications was not the topic.

Include one to three (two is best) examples per KSA. Each example must be unique—do not reuse examples for multiple answers. However, you can subdivide a large project or situation into smaller, specific examples. For example, you can describe your research skills for the background material for a project, analysis you did on a computer, and written reports or oral presentations you made about the project. While these subunits are all part of a larger project, each example highlights a different skill set. Collectively, they could address three or four different KSAs.

Using the CARC formula to write your KSAs

Rest assured, this is not some gimmicky acronym we invented to teach you about KSAs. CARC stands for Context, Action, Result, and Challenge, a proven formula for writing an effective KSA. Federal HR professionals look for these elements in each of your KSAs. This formula works well because it allows your responses to remain focused and to include specific examples.

If your background includes a fair amount of non-academic work experience, you may want to begin your KSA with an introductory paragraph. This paragraph tells the reader how extensive your experience is and quickly goes over how you gained that experience. In other words, it is a quick overview of a specific aspect of your experience. If you lack non-academic experience, you can use this introductory paragraph to quickly summarize how your academic background helped provide you the specific knowledge, skill, or ability you are addressing.

Typically, two paragraphs follow the introductory paragraph. Use each paragraph to give a unique example of applying the specific Knowledge, Skill, and Ability using the CARC formula.

Context: In what job/situation did the example occur? What were the circumstances surrounding the project/problem/opportunity? Were there time/budget/staffing limits?

Action: What did you actually do? Be specific and thorough.

Results: So what happened? If you can, quantify the results with numbers, i.e. savings in dollars, increased productivity, etc. Were there qualitative results like good grades, commendations, or adoption of your procedures? Include positive feedback from superiors, and professors.

Challenge: What was the specific thing you had to do? What made it difficult or challenging? Was there pressure to produce? Did a lot ride on the outcome?

You can use the words "Context, Action, Result and Challenge" in the text of your KSAs, like an outline. It may seem cheesy, but hiring agents are looking for CARC; they will appreciate your attempt to make your application clear and easy-to-read, and their job easier as a result.

CONSIDER USING LISTS

Economy is important. One way to quickly convey experience is to use lists. This works best for KSAs which request an overview of your experience with a category of items. For example: regulations, legislation, computer programs, or statistical tests. You cannot use lists alone to answer a question but can use them to augment a paragraph. For example:
"To complete the census project, I utilized the computer programs Microsoft Word, Excel, PowerPoint and SPSS. "

PULL EXAMPLES FROM YOUR LIFE IF NECESSARY

You know that saying, "Life is what happens while you're making other plans"? You don't have to always draw from work experience! Remember that inspiring speech you gave to a community group? Maybe you used your organizational skills in a volunteer position. Perhaps you gained your automotive repair skills in your own driveway. As long as it's an example that demonstrates the knowledge, skill, or ability being assessed, it's fair game.

Students gain their knowledge, skills and abilities from many sources. Here are some examples:

Class papers	Presentations
Exams with essays or take-home exams	Special projects
Work Study	Internships
Summer jobs	Volunteer positions
Clubs	Student Government
Hobbies	Religious experience
Family life	

STRATEGIES FOR TACKLING MORE COMPLEX KSAs

Some KSAs are more complex than others. A KSA can be as simple as "Ability to Communicate Orally," and other KSAs can be multiple thoughts in one question.

Make sure you fully understand the question. Some KSAs are obvious to the reader, but many are multi-faceted and complex. Make sure you have a clear idea of what every term or keyword in the question really means. To clarify the meaning, go back to the "Duties" section and see how the KSAs support the duties in the job. If there is any question in your mind, ask the Human Resources contact listed on the vacancy announcement to clarify it. Or call someone in your network to translate jargon.

Re-examine your experience and find out if it goes by another name. In Step 5 you learned that the federal government uses job titles which do not always correspond to private-sector job titles, or which are so general that they seem to have no meaning. The same may be true for terms used to describe KSAs. For example, you might have used quality control/quality assurance procedures in your job or in a project, even if no one ever called them that.

Discuss the question with others to get ideas. It's always a good idea to seek a fresh perspective on a problem. Ask your friends, classmates, co-workers or family for ideas on what in your background might help you demonstrate strength in a KSA. Other people can suggest ways to broaden your definition of a skill, or remind you of another experience which could apply. At the very least, talking about your skills with others will be good practice for an interview!

Be realistic. If you honestly do not have any experience in, training for, or knowledge of a specific KSA, you must ask yourself if you are indeed qualified for the job. If you are still determined that this is the job for you, you may proceed knowing that you will need training in certain aspects of the position. Falling short in one KSA will not automatically doom your application, especially if there are several KSAs. Remember that employers advertise for the "ideal" candidate, knowing there may not be anyone out there who fits perfectly. However, if you are unable to answer two or more KSAs with confidence, then you probably are not well qualified for the job.

To address a KSA for which you do not have experience, write about a related experience that shares underlying traits. For example, discuss your ability to learn new things and adapt to new situations, showing to the extent possible how this applies to the specific knowledge, skill, or ability being addressed. Whatever you do, avoid the temptation to embellish your KSAs, even a little. Remember that any statement you make in your KSAs must be supported by your resume.

Bear in mind, also, that the Federal hiring process is designed to identify the best candidates, and Federal agencies are supposed to hire only the best. You may be better off spending the time and effort to look for another vacancy instead of applying for a job for which you are marginally qualified.

HOW ARE KSAs SCORED?

Each KSA is "rated" against a crediting plan that the Human Resources staff and the hiring office develop. The rating, or score, is based on:

- How well you demonstrate your knowledge, skill or ability in that area.
- Your level of skill "usage."
- The examples that you use in your CARC stories.

SKILL USAGE

The way you describe your use of skills has a huge impact on how well your application fares, so choose your words carefully. For example, a KSA which asks about "skill in written communication" will have a scale from barely

acceptable to superior usage. The scale varies according to the job. Be honest and accurate in your presentation, but at the same time present yourself in the best possible light. Your job is to sell yourself to the Federal organization as a top, if not the best, applicant. Someone is going to get this job. Help the agency see why it should be you.

KSA method Rating Scale Interpersonal Skill

Benchmark Level	Level Definition	Level Examples
5	Establishes and maintains ongoing working relationships with management, other employees, internal or external stakeholders, or customers. Remains courteous when discussing information or eliciting highly sensitive or controversial information from people who are reluctant to give it. Effectively handles situations involving a high degree of tension or discomfort involving people who are demonstrating a high degree of hostility or distress.	Presents controversial findings tactfully to irate organization senior management officials regarding shortcomings of a newly installed computer system, software programs, and associated equipment.
4		Mediates disputes concerning system design/architecture, the nature and capacity of data management systems, system resources allocations, or other equally controversial/sensitive matters.
3	Cooperates and works well with management, other employees, or customers, on short-term assignments. Remains courteous when discussing information or eliciting moderately sensitive or controversial information from people who are hesitant to give it. Effectively handles situations involving a moderate degree of tension or discomfort involving people who are demonstrating a moderate degree of hostility or distress.	Courteously and tactfully delivers effective instruction to frustrated customers. Provides technical advice to customers and the public on various types of IT such as communication or security systems, data management procedures or analysis, software engineering, or web development.
2		Familiarizes new employees with administrative procedures and office systems.
1	Cooperates and works well with management, other employees, or customers during brief interactions. Remains courteous when discussing information or eliciting non-sensitive or non-controversial information from people who are willing to give it. Effectively handles situations involving little or no tension, discomfort, hostility, or distress.	Responds courteously to customers' general inquiries. Greets and assists visitors attending a meeting within own organization.

Agency Name:
Department Name:
Position Title, Series, Grade:
Announcement Number:
Candidate: Your Name
Social Security Number: 000-00-0000
Title: Knowledge, Skills & Abilities

Factor 1:
Ability to communicate orally.

Context
I orally presented the culmination of my group's work on the Rwandan genocide to our graduate class in Non-profit Management.

Action 1
To begin the project, my group conducted intensive research on the timeline of events in Rwanda.

Action 2
My research component focused on the management structures of the United Nations. I utilized official documents from multiple international governments and intergovernmental organizations. For the presentation, we developed a summary of events, analysis of the crisis and specific management recommendations.

Action 3
Using PowerPoint, I presented the history of the Rwanda genocide, my analysis of management failures and recommendations for change within the United Nations.

Action 4
I also answered questions from the audience.

Results
My 15-minute presentation was positively received by the class. Many people were moved by the story of Rwanda. They were also shocked when we revealed how simple flaws in management structure led to a travesty of justice. Our presentation received an excellent grade, and our professor complimented me for the clarity and succinct nature of my presentation.

Challenge
The presentation was particularly challenging because, after our team spent months analyzing a very complex problem, I was given 15 minutes to present the problem, our group's analyses, and our recommendations. While we worked collaboratively to sort out the issues and recommendations, in the end, I was left to develop an organized presentation outline and script within the lime limits.

KSA EXAMPLE 2

Agency Name:
Department Name:
Position Title, Series, Grade:
Announcement Number:
Candidate: Your Name
Social Security Number: 000-00-0000
Title: Knowledge, Skills & Abilities

Factor 1: Skill in written communications.

Context

As a final project for my Bachelor of Arts in Communications, I wrote a ten-page marketing plan based on research I conducted on products of the 3M Company. I then selected a new product to feature in the project and submitted the work to a local company. My marketing plan followed an outline I developed and included the following components: Executive Summary, Product Details, Market Description, Sales Outlets, Marketing Calendar, and Conclusion.

Action 1

Each section of the marketing plan required specific research and writing styles. For the Executive Summary, I summarized the plan's main points and provided a brief overview of each section. In Product Details, I incorporated photos of the newly-developed product and provided specific details for Sales Representatives. For Sales Outlets, I researched stores and online outlets in which the product could be sold and gave brief descriptions of their customers and sales potential. The Marketing Calendar featured press release submissions, roll-out dates, print deadlines and exhibitions. The Conclusion brought all of the pieces together in a document that highlighted the important facts and projections.

Action 2

I carefully considered my audience for the plan and adopted writing styles and structures appropriate for each audience, including executives, mid-level managers, marketing specialists and sales representatives I was careful to craft the level of detail in each piece to fit the available time and information needs of its target audience.

Action 3

To create a finished product, I summarized information in charts or tables where necessary and formatted the plan using Microsoft Word and Excel. I used fonts, point size and color to polish the project and make the plan easy-to-read.

Results

The marketing plan received an "A" from my project advisor and fulfilled the requirements of my major. In addition, I presented the plan to the Marketing Department of 3M and components of the plan, including my outline, were adopted by their writers.

Challenge

From a writing standpoint, the marketing plan was a particularl challenge because of the widely diverse audience for its various parts. I had to pitch each segment to a different audience, recognizing that each audience was distinct with respect to the reading time and level of detail it could spend on its part of the plan. This fact required me to give the document extensive attention to detail.

Cover Letters

Cover letters should be limited to one page, and should be well-written and gracious, and express your appreciation for a review of your resume. To get you started, the CD-ROM provides a free template for developing a cover letter.

Cover letters for Federal applications are not substantially different from those for private sector applications. Just as in a private-industry job search, the purpose of a cover letter is to get the employer's attention. Highlight your most outstanding qualifications in your cover letter to make it clear as to why you are the best fit for the job.

Cover letters are a great tool in which to introduce yourself and to provide information that is not normally contained in a resume. There is one problem - Federal agencies increasingly are encouraging only electronic submission of job applications. They do this to speed up the process and reduce the amount of paper documents applicants must send and HR specialists must review.

If the Federal agency encourages electronic submission of all application documents (including your Federal resume), then you will lose the opportunity to use a cover letter. The advice we offer below is based on your being able to submit a cover letter with your application.

Limit your cover letter to one page with three paragraphs or sections in the body of the text. It should be formatted in standard business style, including the agency name and address, announcement number and job title, and contact person, at the top. Address it to a specific person whenever possible.

There are a few differences between Federal and business cover letters. For example, it is not necessary to state where you found the vacancy announcement as you might in a business cover letter. Also, you can use a bulleted list of reasons stating why you are well-suited for the position, as opposed to adhering to paragraph form (see objective 2 on following page).

Three cover letter objectives

1. Communicate your enthusiasm

You want the hiring agent to know that you are highly motivated and hope to attain the position. You can communicate this with an upbeat tone or style. To do this, write a draft and read it out loud enthusiastically. Does it sound right, or does the language you use sound strange when you try to act upbeat while reading it?

No matter how good an actor you might be, the line "In my opinion I have qualifications that make me an appropriate candidate for this position," does not sound natural. Try it. The following line is better and could fit in an upbeat letter, "One reason I am eager to work in this position is that my qualifications exactly match the requirements of the job."

While keeping "upbeat" in mind, you must also remember to maintain a professional image. The line, "I am so well qualified for this position it's amazing!" is over the top. Ask someone else to read your draft of the cover letter and tell you if you have balanced enthusiasm with a professional statement of why you should be hired for the job. Most importantly, keep it personal and true to your personality!

2. Summarize why you are ideal for the job

You can state why you are ideal for the job by literally listing the reasons. Just in case you are unable to think of them, check out this list and see which ones might apply to you:
- Your knowledge, skills, and abilities
- Your experience and training
- Your core competencies, like being able to work independently, in teams, under pressure, or creatively
- Your desire to support the agency mission
- Your desire to work for the particular office
- Your desire to help the particular customer-base
- Your desire to live in that location
- The duties and responsibilities appeal to you
- The position fits into your long-term career goals
- Your desire to serve your country

3. Explain any unusual circumstances.

The last purpose of the cover letter is to explain any unusual circumstances if necessary. These might include gaps in your career timeline, disabilities and accommodations required, conflicts of interest, or anything you think they should know. If you think something on your resume might be considered unusual but you are not certain, you should ask friends in your network if they would include it in the letter.

HOW TO WRITE THE COVER LETTER
Divide your letter into three sections:

Paragraph 1:
- Ask them to accept your application.
- Name the job title, agency, and announcement number.
- In one sentence, summarize why they should hire you.

Paragraph 2:
- Lead-in or introduce the reasons why you are ideal for the job.
- Discuss exactly why you are ideal for the job.
- Write this in paragraph format, or choose an alternative style to list your reasons. A bulleted format works well, if space permits.

Paragraph 3:
- Discuss any unusual circumstances.
- Reiterate your enthusiasm.
- Thank them for accepting your materials.
- Tell them how and where they can contact you if they have any questions.

Conclusion

Writing KSA narratives and cover letters is indeed challenging. KSAs require in-depth thought, research, sometimes creativity, and superior writing skills. Consider KSA writing your golden opportunity to develop your interviewing skills. Cover letters enable you to ask for acceptance of your application, explain those last details, and sell your enthusiasm and personality! Congratulations — you have completed the steps on researching federal jobs and writing an effective application. Go on to Step 8 and Start Applying for Federal Jobs now!

Q&A with the Merit Systems Protection Board

What tips are most important for students to remember when writing KSA's?

"In the first place, students should expect that recruiters are seeing applications almost identical to theirs—same education, same degrees, same grade point averages, etc. The big question is, 'What have they done?' If you have incredible degrees and coursework, recruiters will be looking to see what you've done with it.

"It reflects poorly on your application if you have wonderful credentials but don't show many results or outcomes. Sometimes volunteer work is the best way for students to stand-out. You should always be thinking and challenging yourself during your education to make sure you're actually producing and doing something, not just sitting back passively."

Meredith Jones
B.S. Civil Engineering (Expected May 2006)
Department of Interior, Bureau of Reclamation

I first heard about the Student Career Experience Program (SCEP) when I sat next to someone in one of my classes who worked as a summer intern for the Bureau of Reclamation. When I went to my college's career fair, I visited their booth to learn more about the program. After talking with someone who was a past SCEP student about the program, I left the booth very excited about this opportunity!

I met with a Career Specialist who works with federal jobs at my college career center. She explained some important formatting rules and requirements for government resumes. She also sent me an example resume to follow. I compiled my resume and KSAs and applied for the job. Within a month after applying, following a phone interview, I was offered a job for the summer!

The SCEP internship program allows me to work for two summers or 640 hours and finish school. While in school, the Bureau of Reclamation may pay up to 70 percent of my tuition and books. After I have completed my degree, the agency can offer me a permanent job if I do well in my internship.

Read Meredith's entire Case Study and Success Story on the CD-ROM.

1 2 3 4 5 6 7 **8** 9 10

Federal Job Applications Are Challenging

When applying for Federal jobs, there are two important things to remember: 1) follow the directions on the vacancy announcement, and 2) know the deadline.

The Federal job market is significantly different from the private sector. As we have previously discussed: job terminology varies between the two; Federal resumes are more detailed and complex to prepare, there are often essay questions you must answer, and a response to your Federal application can take months. At first glance this can be intimidating. Novice Federal jobseekers may try to use materials they have prepared for the private sector, but they won't get far.

One reason the Federal job search process is so exhaustive is that your application package represents an examination (with actual grading) of your qualifications. Consider this: to apply for a job in the private sector you submit a cover letter, a basic resume, and maybe a form or two. You may be called in for a screening interview, and subsequently return for another one or two interviews that progressively provide the organization with more information regarding your experience and qualifications.

The Federal job application process entails revealing more about yourself in the initial application. For instance, you may answer up to 150 yes/no questions (on the Form C), or answer 27 (more or less) multiple choice questions, give 7 examples (short KSAs), and submit a Federal resume. First, the Human Resources recruiters will review the packages to determine who are the best qualified candidates. And then second, your resume might be forwarded to the supervisor who will possibly set up an interview. In this more lengthy two-step review process, the Federal government can more effectively screen applications to find the most qualified person for the job. One source of confusion for novice Federal jobseekers is not truly understanding the multiple job application systems the government uses. As introduced in Step 5 (Finding Vacancy Announcements), right now about half of all automated Federal applications are processed using question-driven automated systems such as Avue, COOL, QuickHire, or USAStaffing, and the rest are processed using the resume-driven system called Resumix®, Despite the Federal government's emphasis on automation, many agencies are not yet using technology to process job applications, and there are still many situations where paper applications are used. The good news is that with your one good resume, and by familiarizing yourself with the systems, you can apply for many jobs quickly and relatively easily.

Follow the Directions on the Vacancy Announcement

Never deviate from the written instructions on a Federal vacancy announcement for any reason. Even if you speak to someone in the Human Resources department and they tell you to do something different, don't do it. Here's why:

> "I wanted to apply for a job under a special career intern program. The instructions were a little unusual, so I called the HR office to ask a question. They wanted two letters of recommendation, and I wasn't sure who would be most appropriate to get one of the letters from. The person I talked to put me a hold for a second, then came back and said that one letter was actually sufficient, if it addressed the two questions asked. So that's what I did. Then my application got rejected because it was incomplete! When I complained, the office manager said she didn't know why anyone would tell me to submit only one letter. I never got the name of the person I originally talked to, but it wouldn't make any difference now." - Anonymous jobseeker

Although this kind of horror story is rare, we can still learn from it. Always ask the name of the person you speak with in Human Resources in case there's a problem down the line. But more importantly, if you deviate from the instructions, your application may not be considered. Read the instructions carefully, make sure you know when and how to apply and what to submit.

Know the Deadline

Applications for Federal job vacancies will be accepted only while the vacancy is "open." Open periods can be as short as a few days or as long as several weeks. These are set by the agencies, and represent your window for applying for the job. The closing date is the last day applications will be accepted. It will be clearly indicated on the announcement.

If you happen to find a vacancy announcement at the last minute, that you just have to apply for, the exact time of day on the closing date can be important. Many vacancy announcements, especially those on web-based systems, close at midnight on the deadline. Be mindful of how the date and time is expressed. The database for QuickHire is maintained in Alexandria, VA, and the closing time is usually expressed in terms of Eastern Time (Standard or Daylight Savings).

Some announcements that require emailed or faxed applications, close at 5 p.m. on the deadline. Others need to be postmarked on that day. If you are mailing your application, you will want to know if your package must be received or postmarked by the closing date. The difference between these two is huge. Often, supplemental materials, like transcripts, can be submitted shortly after the closing date.

Some vacancy announcements have open periods that are months long, years long, are "open until filled," or are indefinitely open. These are called "inventory-building" announcements and generally are used when an agency expects to fill many jobs over a long period of time. Resumes from qualified applicants are collected in a file, and when a specific job opens up, the file is reviewed. The inventory-building announcements are effective for the HR recruiters because the candidates have their resumes posted and ready for review.

Package What They Want

Paper Packages: The appearance of your application is important. If you are applying via a paper package, use good quality bond paper. White is customary, but you may use ivory colored paper. Your cover letter, resume, and KSAs should be separate documents. Transcripts can be photocopies and do not need to be official copies. Package your documents in a large envelope so that they do not have to be folded.

On-Line Applications: For electronic applications, complete all of the pages and questions. Make sure you finish the submission. Sometimes there are at least 3 steps to applying: Profile/Registration; Resume Builder or Resume Submission; Questions or Essays. Be sure you are not exceeding the maximum number of characters allowed in a field. There's very little formatting that you can do within text fields, but make entries as easy to read as possible.

Combination Online and Fax: If you are asked to apply on-line, but then fax additional information, make sure you include your SSN, name and announcement number on each paper submitted by fax. You could add a cover letter to the faxed information.

How to apply to agencies using paper applications

Agencies that are still using paper applications may allow several options for your application format. The package usually contains the following: Cover letter, Federal Resume, KSAs, supplemental information (such as transcripts).

The package is usually mailed, faxed, or hand delivered. You may use the U.S. Postal Service, or other delivery method to transport your package.

Here's a nice clear set of instructions from a vacancy announcement:

> *"Your application will consist of three components. The first component consists of your statement addressing how you meet each of the knowledge, skills or abilities listed for this vacancy. The second component is your Resume. The final component of your application consists of "other" application materials. Examples of these other materials include your college transcripts (if required) and documentation of veteran status (if applicable). Instructions on completing and submitting these items follow."*

We recommend that you use the preferred paper format, a Federal resume. Also in the announcement, usually at the end, is the address to which to send your materials, a number to which to fax it, and perhaps instructions on how to apply with email. If you mail your application, we recommend that you get a return receipt. If you are facing a deadline, fax or email will deliver your application the same day.

Your paper application should include the following:

1. A nicely formatted Federal resume printed on good quality paper
2. KSA narratives (a separate document)
3. A cover letter.
4. Include copies of required supplemental information such as photocopies of transcripts.

How to apply to agencies using Automated Recruitment Systems

Refer to the charts and screenshots from Step 5 for detailed information on what is required for various automated application systems.

Federal agencies have choices in how to manage their candidates' resumes and other applications. Most agencies have chosen to use automation to help them, but a few have not. For agencies that do not use automated systems, on-line application is not possible.

Those using automation can choose among developing their own systems, using a system developed by the Office of Personnel Management, or buying or leasing any of several on-line application systems developed by private companies. Agencies are prohibited from requiring someone to apply electronically, but most agencies with electronic capability will strongly encourage you (and help you if necessary) to submit your application on-line.

The automated systems that agencies use fall into two broad categories that, for our purposes, we will call "question-driven" and "resume-driven." Here is a run-down on the systems that were in use when we went to press:

QUESTION-DRIVEN SYSTEMS:

This includes the following commercial and government-developed systems presented in alphabetical name order. These are similar but not exactly the same with respect to their look, feel, and job application process. A defining characteristic of this group is that they rely heavily on multiple-choice and "yes-no" questions to make distinctions among job applicants.

AvueCentral™ – This commercial system is used by more than 12 agencies, including the U.S. Forest Service and U.S. Coast Guard. This application is a complex on-line form with questions and a profile. You submit your resume one time, then apply for many positions in the database that AvueCentral maintains. However, this can only be done for vacancies in agencies using this system.

> ➲**Quick Tip:** Copy and paste your resume information into the AvueCentral database. See page 117.

eRecruit™ - This commercial system is used by NSA, and parts of the Department of Homeland Security. The significant features of this system are its on-line form screens and questions. Plus, it offers a shopping cart for selecting your target careers.

> ➲**Quick Tip:** Attach your Resume Builder resume for the eRecruit system. See page 117.

QuickHire™ (A government solution by Monster.com) - This system is currently used by about 40 federal agencies. You will complete a profile, insert your resume information into the online field, answer registration questions, and respond to job-related questions (yes/no and multiple choice). In many instances your answer will trigger a box in which you will be asked to provide a short essay explaining your answer or demonstrating what experience, education, or training you have to support the answer you gave.

> ➲**Quick Tip:** Copy and paste your resume into the Flexible Electronic Field format. See the sample on page 119.

USAStaffing™ This automated system was developed by the Office of Personnel Management. Agencies may purchase the right to use the system themselves, or may contract OPM to manage the system for them (conduct the recruiting and prepare the lists of qualified job candidates). You will recognize announcements prepared by this system because of their "Form C" questionnaires, which typically range from 27 to 156 multiple-choice or yes/no questions.

> ➲ **Quick Tip:** Use either the Resume Builder or Flexible Resume for this system. You may copy and paste the text into the online fields.

RESUME-DRIVEN SYSTEM:

Resumix™ (Owned by Hotjobs.com) - This is the only "keyword" system used by government agencies. This system is used by NASA and all components of the Department of Defense (including Army, Air Force, and Navy). This system is used by submitting information into a complex resume builder, answering personnel questions in a Supplemental Data Sheet, and "self-nominating" for specific vacancies. A major distinction between Resumix™ and the question-driven systems is that Resumix™ does not use a series of questions to assess your qualifications. Instead, it applies artificial intelligence to "read" resumes and distinguishes among applicants through words and phrases included in their resumes.

> ➲ **Quick Tip:** Use Resume Builder format for Resumix. See the sample on page 117.

Timing: How long does it take to get hired?

Currently, the waiting time is likely to be 2 to 4 months. The following chart illustrates the path of your resume from the initial review system to the supervisor who can decide to interview you for the position.

HOW FEDERAL JOB APPLICATIONS ARE PROCESSED CHART

Key steps in Federal hiring that involve job applicants interaction

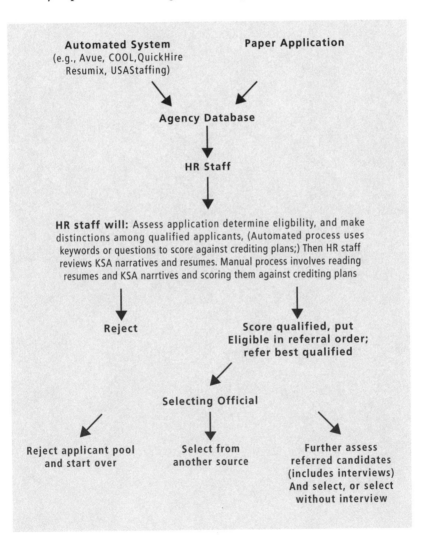

Automated System
(e.g., Avue, COOL,QuickHire
Resumix, USAStaffing)

Paper Application

Agency Database

HR Staff

HR staff will: Assess application determine eligbility, and make distinctions among qualified applicants, (Automated process uses keywords or questions to score against crediting plans;) Then HR staff reviews KSA narratives and resumes. Manual process involves reading resumes and KSA narrtives and scoring them against crediting plans

Reject

Score qualified, put Eligible in referral order; refer best qualified

Selecting Official

Reject applicant pool and start over

Select from another source

Further assess referred candidates (includes interviews) And select, or select without interview

Conclusion

In addition to preparing a well-written resume and KSA narratives, knowing how to apply for federal jobs increases your likelihood of successfully landing a Federal job. A smart Federal jobseeker will apply for many jobs and internships to broaden his/her chances of finding that ideal job. Step 9 will show you how to Track and Follow-up Applications!

Scott Hampstead
B.S., Mechanical Engineering
Career Management Internship, GS-0830-07
U.S. Army Corps of Engineers, Baltimore District

My advice for accomplishing a successful Federal job search is this: Don't be afraid to write an email to the HR person listed on the announcement. Strategize, communicate, ask questions, follow-up. Keep the emails short, but by all means ask about the status of your application. This communication can help humanize the application process. I wrote a number of emails during my 3-month waiting process (which felt like a year!). I was hired by one agency, but preferred another. So I wrote to the second agency and told them that I was offered a job by the first agency, but that I really wanted to work for them. IT WORKED! They got their applications moving and I got an offer from the second agency within a month. I felt that communicating with the HR person and the hiring manager was critical to staying on top of the application process and, as a result, landed my Internship.

During my Career Management Internship position with the Baltimore District, I will be receiving rotational training, obtaining a Security Clearance, and will be earning $47,000 after six months. The benefits and work atmosphere are excellent and the opportunity to learn is amazing. In my search for engineering positions in the Army and Navy, I was offered an opportunity to apply for a Security Clearance, which will be invaluable during my entire Engineering career.

Read Scott's Resumix on the CD-ROM.

1 2 3 4 5 6 7 8 **9** 10

You mean I can contact them?

Most Federal job applicants are not aware that they can contact the HR personnel handling their application. Asking questions, gaining information, developing a relationships, becoming known are a helpful part of the application process. You can track and follow-up most of the steps your application follows through the system. Some of the online application systems are even set up to ensure that you will be contacted.

Vacancy announcements typically include the name of a Human Resources contact who is responsible for many aspects of the application process. This HR person may have created the vacancy announcement, posted it on USAJobs and other websites, and may communicate with the hiring supervisor. They may coordinate the review of the packages and be part of the rating and ranking process to determine who will get an interview. This HR person is a great resource for you. Refer back to the Federal Hiring Chart in Step 8 on page 151 to review how central this HR person is in the process!

Just a reminder, they are busy!
Human resources staff are occupied with multiple announcements, various aspects of announcement development, reviewing packages, and responding to supervisor needs. Use diplomacy and consideration when contacting them about your package. Your goal is to be remembered favorably!

How long does it take?
The Office of Personnel Management recently wrote a memo asking the agencies to speed up their hiring process to a total of 45 days, from the closing date of the announcement to the interview date. Merit principles, which guide Federal hiring practices, mandate detailed and thorough processing of applications. And yes, they do want to hire the best possible new employees!

Play the Application Game

The best philosophy here is to learn all that you can about the jobs and internships that are a good fit for your degree, experience, location, salary and interests. Make sure your Federal resume and KSAs include keywords for your target jobs! Apply for as many of these positions and internships as you can find. Manage your campaign by tracking your application and follow-up. In about 30 days, you will be receiving "hits." The sheer volume of your effort and energy will pay off.

How can you contact the HR person?

- ⮱ **Telephone:** You probably won't reach the HR person with your first call, so be ready with a good voicemail message. Practice your message before calling.
- ⮱ **What if you try calling and there is continually no answer?** If the phone is always busy, or you leave a voicemail and never receive a call back, here's what you can do: Research another vacancy announcement with the same agency (preferably at the same grade level), look for a contact name and phone on that announcement and call him or her. They are probably co-workers and this person may be able to tell you what happened to the recruiter you are seeking. It's possible that they changed jobs, are on vacation, or are on detail to another agency. HR staff people are usually very helpful and informative. And, they may be able to answer your question themselves.
- ⮱ **Email:** By all means, use this method if it is recommended.
- ⮱ **Fax:** Sometimes only a fax number is provided. In this case, write inquiries simply and clearly, making sure to include your contact information.
- ⮱ **No personal contact information:** If there is no name or personal contact information, but there is an address, you may write a letter. If there is no address, but a database, you cannot contact anyone. Just submit your application and cross your fingers.

Suggested telephone, email and fax scripts to track and follow-up your application

1st Message – 30 days after the closing date
"Hi, Ms. Rogers, this is Emily Troutman from San Diego, CA. I'm inquiring about my application for Writer-Editor, GS-7, announcement 20205, which I submitted on April 5, 20xx. I'd like to know the status of my package, or when the packages are being reviewed. Can you please return my call, or leave a voicemail at (410) 777-7777. The best time to reach me is 8 to 10 am. Thank you."

2nd Message –
2 to 4 weeks after the HR person responds to your message by voicemail
"Hi, Ms. Rogers, this is Emily Troutman again. Thanks for your voicemail on Monday, April 9th regarding announcement 20205, Writer-Editor. I'm checking again on the status of my application. I am still very interested in the job, but other opportunities are appearing. I hope that a decision will be made soon, and that I am going to be interviewed. I want this job and I believe I can make a positive contribution to your agency. I need a job and I've been looking 6 months. My voicemail again is (410) 777-7777."

3rd Contact –
2 to 4 weeks after the 2nd contact (this time make it by fax or email)
To: Susan Rogers, HR Staff for Announcement 20205, Writer-Editor
From: Emily Troutman, SSN 220-00-0000
Re: Position of Writer-Editor, Closing Date April 5, 20xx

Hello, Ms. Rogers, I'm still hopeful that I'm in the list of Best Qualified Candidates for this position. I've been reading about your agency in the newspaper and see that there are new programs for housing and construction. I would be able to start immediately.
Can you please let me know if this position still exists? I am determined to get a federal job, and I really like the mission of your agency. I could contribute a lot and be very effective there. If another person has been selected, I'd really like to know so that I can pursue other positions. Thanks so much for your help. I look forward to your call. My phone is (410) 777-7777. The best time to reach me is 8 to 10 am."

YOU'VE BEEN TOLD YOU'RE NOT GETTING THE JOB (Telephone)

"Hello, Ms. Rogers, This is Emily Troutman. I got the notice that I was not hired for the job (Announcement 20205, Writer-Editor). When you have a few minutes, I would really appreciate your help with knowing why I was not selected. I'd really like to work for the government in your agency and I felt I was perfectly qualified. If you could take a few minutes and call me back or leave a voicemail, I would appreciate knowing what I could do improve in my resume or my qualifications for future applications. Thanks so much for your help. My number is 410-777-7777. The best time to reach me is 8 to 10 am."

YOU'RE GETTING AN INTERVIEW – Congratulations! (Telephone)

"Hello, Ms. Rogers, this is Emily Troutman, Thanks so much for the opportunity to interview for the Writer-Editor job, announcement 20205. I am very pleased! I would like to know if you can give me some insight into the interview system. Will there be one person or a panel interviewing me? Also, will the interview follow specific questions? And if so, would I be able to receive these questions ahead of time? I am beginning my research and preparation for the interview now! I look forward to this opportunity. Thanks for any information you can provide! My number is 410-777-7777. The best time to reach me is 8 to 10 am."

AFTER THE INTERVIEW – THANK YOU NOTE!

Dear Ms. Rogers:
Thank you so much for your time last Wednesday. I enjoyed meeting you and hearing about your agency. I believe that I would be an asset to your organization and feel certain that I would be able to learn quickly about your mission and programs. I look forward to your decision and hope that I can begin my career at the Office of _____ at Department of _____.

Thank you again,
Sincerely, Emily Troutman

Sample Questions for applicants to ask Human Resources:

1. Can you clarify something from the announcement for me?
If you don't understand exactly a certain request of the vacancy announcement, ask for clarification. If the person you're talking to isn't the named contact person, be sure to get his or her name.

2. Have you received all my materials?
Many vacancy announcements require you to submit materials by different methods. For example, you may have to use a USAStaffing online application system which follows two steps: 1) submit information on-line, and 2) fax or mail your transcripts. It's a good idea to check to see if all your materials have been received before the closing date. Some electronic application systems, like COOL, list the status of your application materials. If you mail any materials, remember to save your receipts.

3. What is the status of my application?
The federal job application process can take a while. You can call to check on the status of your application, but we suggest that you wait about a month after the closing date. You may learn that you did or did not get on the list submitted to the selecting official, or that interviews are being conducted.

4. How can I improve future applications?
This is REALLY IMPORTANT. If you learn that you didn't get referred for a position, ask the contact person to tell you what you should do to improve future applications. You may learn that you missed a selective factor. You may learn that you weren't qualified for a particular grade. You may learn that you didn't score highly on your KSAs. You may also learn that you scored very well, but were in competition with a highly qualified group of applicants.

The HR representative usually will not go into great detail, but may tell you what your overall score was, where your KSA's were weak, and where you ranked among the pool of applicants. If you didn't get the job you were seeking, then talking on the phone with the people who read and scored your materials can be the most valuable five or ten minutes you can spend in this whole process.

Conclusion

The more jobs and internships you can find to apply for, the better. With the government's response time to applications, it is better if you keep applying. If you receive an interview from one announcement, but really prefer another job, then you will have to decide what to do. What a good problem to have! The more packages you submit, the better your chances will be of having interviews and being considered for jobs. In Step 10, you will learn how to interview for a federal job.

INTERVIEW FOR A FEDERAL JOB

David F. Raikow, Ph. D.
Research Aquatic Biologist, GS-0401-11
National Oceanic and Atmospheric Administration

I've had two Federal interviews, first for an EPA GS-9 and the other the NOAA GS-11 position I landed. The GS-9 interview was a 3-on-1 panel type. One person took the lead and asked most of the questions. They used a combination of question types: 1) open-ended questions that forced me to describe myself professionally and the kind of experience I had, and 2) specific fact-based questions to see if I knew what I was talking about and if I had done some homework.

My visit lasted about 90 minutes from the time I arrived early to the time I left after brief post-interview chit-chat. The actual interview was close to an hour. The lead interviewer took copious notes. I didn't have any trouble answering the questions until they got to the part where they asked me why I, a Ph. D., would want a GS-9 position with no promotion potential (I qualified to start at GS-11). The most truthful answer was because I needed a job, plain and simple, but I just couldn't see saying something like "Hey, its better than unemployment." What I told them was that this job was a chance to use my skills to support the mission of EPA, which honestly was important to me.

Read the rest of David's interview experiences in his Case Study on the CD-ROM

1 2 3 4 5 6 7 8 9 **10**

Congratulations!
You have been selected for an interview!

The Federal government uses many different approaches to interviewing. This section will help you understand these approaches and provide some practical tips on preparing for interviews.

Managers vary their interviewing techniques and processes to develop an understanding of you as a candidate for their position. The interview will depend on the type of position, as well as the information the manager needs to obtain to determine if you are the best "fit" for the position.

Interviews for students or interns may be, in many ways, no different from regular employment interviews. You may be asked about long-term career goals, your interest in the position and the agency, and your long- and short-term education plans. Be ready to discuss your current or previous courses and what you are learning in a relevant manner!

Interviews may be conducted in person or over the phone, and may include an interview panel. Interview elements may include several categories, including:

- ➱ Behavioral
- ➱ Technical
- ➱ Competency

All of the interview methods listed above call for some preparation on your part. However, you need to understand which type of interview you will be participating in. When you are contacted for the interview, it is appropriate for you to request information regarding the type and method of interviewing that will be conducted.

Let's discuss the different interviewing methods listed above.

Behavioral Interviewing:
This is an employment interview, situational in nature, designed to see how interviewees will respond to different situations. Behavioral interviews are designed to help forecast your future behavior on the job, based on your past behaviors in different situations.

Your supervisor has left an assignment for you, but has left on vacation for a week. The assignment is due when she returns. You don't completely understand the assignment – what would you do?

You have been responsible for dealing with a particularly challenging client, who has indicated in their latest phone call, that they are thinking of taking their business some place else. How would you handle the situation?

The successful candidate for this position will be working with some highly-trained individuals who have been with the organization for a long time. How will you approach them?

Tell me about a time when you took it upon yourself to accomplish a task on the job without being asked.

Describe a major obstacle you have overcome.

Tips for Preparing for a behavioral interview:
> Prior to the interview, spend some time identifying behaviors that would be critical to success in the position – and do an honest assessment!

> Do a "google" and look for behavioral interview questions – and practice!

> Spend some time thinking through mistakes you have made in the workplace – what would you do differently – in other words, how would you change your behavior the next time?

Technical Interviewing:
Technical interviews are focused on providing the selecting official with additional information regarding the technical or functional skills of the applicant.

Describe your experience with accounting principles, practices, and techniques.

Describe your experience in applying program management theories and processes.

This position requires experience in scientific research – provide us with information on your role and/or participation in performing basic and/or applied research.

How do you keep abreast of new developments in your profession or industry? On a scale of 1-10, how up to date are you?

How does your degree in (major) prepare you for a career in (occupation/industry), or to excel as a (position title).

In your current job/school situation, what types of decisions do you make without consulting your immediate supervisor?

On a scale on 1-5, how would you assess your technical skills and why?

Tips for Preparing for a technical interview:
>   Closely review the technical requirements listed in the vacancy announcement, and develop a mental inventory of your skills for each requirement.

>   Identify questions you may have regarding the technical requirements of the work – this will demonstrate your ability to prepare as well as your technical skill level.

>   Check with college professors, peers and counselors regarding information on the technical challenges and issues facing the organization; develop scenarios for problem-solving!

Competency Interviewing:

An employment interview in which the competencies have been defined by the organization, and in which applicants are asked questions to determine their possession of the competencies required for the position. These interviews may seem like the behavioral interview described above.

Describe a time when you were under pressure to make a decision. How did you react?

Can you think of a problem or situation that you have encountered, where the old solutions simply didn't work, and when you came up with a new solution(s).

Are you a risk-taker or do you prefer to play it safe?

What changes have you made in your life and why? Which are you most proud of?

Tips for preparing for a competency interview:

Spend some time thinking about mistakes you have made on the job or in school – how would you explain them to an interviewer – and what have you learned from those mistakes.

Research the organization's website to identify organizational competencies and values, and assess how you would fit in to the organization.

Research practice questions and work with peers or counselors to practice responding to questions.

Interview Tips

Before the Interview:

- Be prepared!
- Check out the website of the agency you're interviewing with and conduct research (size, services, products, etc.).
- Prepare a one-minute response to the "Tell me about yourself" question.
- Be memorable! Media training expert TJ Walker from www.worldwidemedia.com recommends that you have a story or message prepared so that you will be remembered at the "water cooler."
- Try to find out what kind of interview to expect, i.e. behavioral, technical, etc. Feel free to ask when scheduling the interview.
- Write five success stories to answer behavioral interview questions, ("Tell me about a time when…" or "Give me an example of a time…").
- Prepare answers to the most common interview questions that will best present your skills, talents, and accomplishments:
  - Why did you leave your last position?
  - What do you know about our organization?
  - What are your goals/Where do you see yourself in 5 years?
  - What are your strengths and weaknesses?
  - Why would you like to work for this organization?
  - What is your most significant achievement?
  - How would your last boss and colleagues describe you?
  - Why should we hire you?
  - What are your salary expectations?
- Remember nothing will make you look worse than not knowing what you put on your own resume.
- Have 10 questions prepared for the interviewer. Only ask the ones which were not addressed during your discussion.
- Practice in front of a mirror or with a friend for feedback.
- Have your references' permission. These might be former managers, professors, friends of your family (but not family members), or people who know you through community service. You want them to be prepared to praise you. It would be beneficial to provide your references with the following information: the job for which you are applying, the name of the organization, and a copy of your resume.

The Interview:

- Arrive 10 to 15 minutes early for your interview.
- Dress appropriately! Ironed clothes, including skirts (at knee length or longer), nice slacks or suit. Keep your interview outfit simple and professional. Be conservative (until you get hired).
- Carry these items to the interview:
    - A copy of your references (for which you already have permission);
    - Paper on which to take notes;
    - Directions to the interview site;
    - A copy of your resume;
    - Pen;
- Be aware of your body language and eye contact. Stand and greet your interviewer with a firm handshake and a smile. Crossed-arms appear to be defensive, fidgeting may make everyone nervous, and lack of eye contact may be interpreted as an untrustworthy person. Instead, nod while listening to show you are attentive and alert, and most importantly, sit and stand upright.
- Think before you answer; if you do not have a clear understanding a question, ask for clarification.
- Express yourself clearly and with confidence, not conceit. Keep your answers concise and to the point.
- Show a sincere interest in the office and position. (You already know about the organization, as you already conducted your research.)
- Focus on what you can contribute to the organization rather than what the employer can do for you. Don't ask about salary or benefits until the employer brings it up.
- Try not to talk about politics (don't bring it up yourself). Talk about your skills and experience, but don't start a political discussion.
- Do not place blame on or be negative about past employers.
- End the interview on an positive note indicating how you feel you are a good fit for the position at hand, and how you can make a contribution to the organization. Ask about the next step, as most offers are not extended on the spot.
- Thank the interviewer and ask for a business card (this will provide you with the necessary contact information).

After the Interview:
Thank you letters should be written graciously, promptly, and carefully.
Think about the best form for your thank you. If the interviewer tells you
he/she plans to make a decision that night, then you should e-mail promptly.
At the same time, if you are applying to an agency that prides itself on
doing personalized work for clients, you may want to send a handwritten
message on a nice card. Either way, thank the interviewer for his/her time,
gently reminding them of your interest in the position, and the valuable
contributions you would bring to the organization. Do not miss that last
chance to market yourself!

Conclusion:

An interview is not the final destination on your federal job search—it's the
beginning of your federal career. It's also a chance to think back to Step One,
Networking. Job interviews are a great way to meet people on the inside,
whether or not you get the job. If your interviewer takes a genuine interest
in you, ask if you can keep in touch and let them know where you end up.
Always send a thank-you note and let them know if you're still on the market.
Since they know your qualifications, they may keep you in mind for other
job announcements or be willing to provide references. One interview may
be the beginning of a great mentoring relationship or open the doors to
opportunity in the future.

Final Words:

"In today's world of danger and opportunity, there is no higher calling than public service. No other job affords you the chance to impact people's lives for the better, promote their safety and health, and open access to public services. From my own experience, I can attest to the satisfaction that Federal service can bring to employees who know they are making a difference for the good in the lives of others. This book has been intended for those students who are thinking about Federal employment for the first time. I hope that it helps open the door to this world and sheds light on the paths to the kind of satisfaction I took from my own career in Federal Service."

The Honorable Alvin P. Adams
Former Ambassador to Peru and Haiti

GLOSSARY:
STUDENT'S FEDERAL CAREER GUIDE

1 2 3 4 5 6 7 8 9 10

A

Ability (as in Knowledge, Skills and Abilities - KSAs) The demonstrated capability to perform an observable behavior or a behavior that results in an observable product.

Applicant A person who applies for a vacant position. (Thus, merely completing an on-line resume and providing personal information, without actually applying for a specific announced vacancy, does not make an applicant.)

Appointee A person who is appointed to a position, and who enters into duty with the hiring agency.

Appointing Authority The legal or regulatory basis upon which an appointment may be made to a Federal civilian position.

Appointing Officer A person having the authority, by law, or by duly delegated authority, to appoint, employ, or promote individuals to positions in an agency.

Assessment A method of evaluating a candidate's job-related competencies/ KSAs using multiple raters and exercises to evaluate each competency. Assessment centers use various competency-related assessment simulations, including group exercises, in-basket exercises, questionnaires, fact-finding exercises, interviews, and role-playing.

Assessment Tool A device or method used to measure the degree to which an applicant possesses the competencies or KSAs necessary for successful job performance. Written tests, rating schedules, work samples, and structured interviews are all examples of assessment tools.

Avue Central The name of a commercial company and of the trademarked automated hiring process that it has developed and that is used by a number of Federal agencies. This automated system receives, tracks, and rates applications.

Augmentation A procedure by which additional points are added to the ratings of eligibles based upon an assessment of competencies/KSAs pertaining to specific job-related criteria that were not previously measured.

B

Behavioral Consistency Method A method of assessing a person's training and experience by asking candidates to describe their major achievements in several job-related areas identified for the position, called job dimensions (i.e., competencies/KSAs). It operates on the assumption that past behavior is the best predictor of future performance.

Bilingual/ Bicultural Certification A special hiring program established under the Luevano Consent Decree to hire eligible applicants who meet the program's special criteria (proficiency in both the English and Spanish languages or knowledge of Hispanic culture) into positions where that proficiency or knowledge is beneficial.

C

Candidate An applicant who meets the minimum qualifications requirements for a position, and thus is eligible for employment consideration. See also "Eligible."

Career Conditional Appointment Appointment to a non-temporary position in the competitive service. This is the most common kind of appointment for new hires entering the civil service through competitive procedures.

Career Transition Assistance Program (CTAP) A program designed by an agency to actively assist its surplus and displaced employees by providing selection priority for competitive service vacancies. This program requires agencies to notify its affected of its plans to fill vacancies in their local commuting areas.

Case Examining A hiring technique where job-seekers apply directly for a specific job and are rated and ranked using job-related competencies/ KSAs. Following the examination process a certificate of eligibles is prepared for the vacant position, but a standing inventory of qualified applicants is not prepared.

Category Rating A process of assessing qualified eligibles by quality categories rather than by discrete numeric scores. An agency using category rating assesses candidates against job-related criteria and then places them into two or more pre-defined categories.

Certificate of Eligibles (Also called "Certificate") A list of the highest-ranked eligibles in score and in veteran's preference order. It is given to a selecting official who considers the named eligibles for appointment consideration in accordance with competitive selection laws and regulations.

Closing Date The date beyond which applications for an advertised position will no longer be accepted. Each vacancy should have a closing date, and that closing date must be stated in the job vacancy announcement for the position.

Competency A measurable pattern of knowledge, skills, abilities, behaviors, and other characteristics that an individual needs to perform work roles or occupational functions successfully.

Competency-Based Job Profile A statement of the general and technical competencies required for optimal performance in an occupation or job family. Competencies determined to be critical for a job provide a basis for developing applicant assessments.

Competitive Appointment An appointment based on selection from a competitive examination or under other specific authority.

Competitive Examining (1) The process used to fill civil service positions with candidates who apply from outside the Federal workforce. It is also used to enable current Federal employees without civil service status to compete for permanent appointments and to enable employees with civil service status to compete for other Federal positions. (2) A competitive examination, which is open to all applicants, may consist of a written test, an evaluation of an applicant's education and experience, and/or an evaluation of other attributes necessary for successful performance in the position to be filled.

Competitive Status An acquired designation that represents a person's basic eligibility for assignment (for example, by transfer, promotion, reassignment, demotion, or reinstatement) to a position in the competitive service without having to compete with members of the general public in an open competitive examination. Once acquired, status belongs to the individual, not to the position.

Competitor Inventory A competitor inventory is a rank-ordered list of eligibles who meet one set of qualification requirements, have passed one examining vehicle, and are available to be considered for: one or more grade levels; one or more occupational specialties; at one or more geographical locations; and various employment conditions identified on the job announcement such as, travel, night or shift work. A competitor inventory is an alternative to case examining.

Content Validity A characteristic possessed by an assessment instrument the contents of which accurately reflect actual job requirements. A typing test is an example of an assessment instrument that would likely have high content validity for assessing qualifications to be a clerk-typist. Also referred to as "face validity."

COOL (Commerce Opportunities On-Line) The name of an automated hiring process developed and used by the Department of Commerce. It is used to receive, track, and rate applications. As this book was being written, the Department of Commerce was considering replacing COOL with a commercial automated system.

Crediting Plan A method by which a candidate's job-related competencies/ KSAs are assessed by reviewing the factual backgrounds of candidates, to include positions held, levels of responsibility, accomplishments, and the job-related education they have received. Also called a "rating schedule."

Critical Hiring Need A need to fill a particular position or group of positions to meet agency mission requirements brought about by an emergency or potential threat; to meet an unanticipated or unusual mission requirement; to conform to the requirements of law, a Presidential directive or Administration initiative; or to address an unexpected event outside of an agency's control.

Cut-off-Date A date set by an agency after which applications will continue to be accepted, but will not be given initial consideration. It is not the same as a "closing date," but rather establishes an early consideration period. A cut-off date may be useful where large numbers of applications are expected over an extended period of time, and there is an immediate need to fill a position. If a cut-off date is established, it must be stated in the job announcement advertising the position. If a cut-off date is established, an agency must rate, rank, and refer to the selecting official all applications received by that date. In addition, an agency must consider any application received from a 10-point preference eligible who applies after the cut-off date but before the date that the certificate is issued. Agencies may consider applications received after the cut-off date only when the initial applicant group is exhausted and/or there are additional vacancies to fill.

D

Deferred-Rated Competitor Inventory This is a list of applicants in alphabetical or identification number order. The list also includes options and grades for which the applicants are considered. Although applications in this inventory may have undergone an initial screening for basic qualifications, they are rated only when a certificate is requested for a specific job announcement. Typically, the rating is valid only for that specific position.

Delegated Examining Authority Authority to fill competitive civil service positions pursuant to a delegation agreement. Delegated examining authority must be exercised in accordance with civil service laws and regulations.

DEO Examiners/ Staff Agency representative(s) or staff member(s) who carry out an agency's delegated examining authority.

Direct-Hire Authority Authority that permits hiring without regard to the provisions of law and regulation that normally give certain veterans, or family members of those veterans, preference in hiring, that prescribe the ordering on and selection of names from a certificate of eligibles that govern the passing over of a veteran, and that govern the normal rules for rating applications. Direct hire authority is permitted when OPM determines either that a severe shortage of candidates or critical hiring need for a position exists.

Displaced Employee A current agency employee serving under a competitive service appointment who meets certain tenure requirements and who has received a specific reduction in force (RIF) separation notice, or notice of proposed removal for declining a directed reassignment or transfer of function outside of the local commuting area.

Dual Certification The concurrent referral of an applicant to more than one position, such as multiple grades, specialties, and/or geographic locations, from eligibility established under a particular job announcement or application procedure.

E

Education Education is an indicator of proficiency that relates to course work the candidate completed that is related to the competencies/KSAs needed to perform in the job.

Eligible An applicant who satisfies the minimum qualifications requirements for the position, and therefore is eligible for employment consideration. See also "Candidate."

Excepted Service A term used to describe all civil service positions that are not in the competitive service or the Senior Executive Service. (See 5 CFR Part 213)

Experience Experience is an indicator of proficiency that relates to the school, home, community, voluntary or work experiences of the candidate that are related to the competencies/KSAs needed to perform in the job.

F

Federal Career Intern Program A special hiring program designed to help agencies recruit and attract exceptional individuals into a variety of occupations. Agencies develop their own programs consistent with OPM regulations. This is a 2-year program in the excepted service intended to provide developmental activities as well as regular work assignments. Appointment is normally at GS-5, -7, or -9. At the agency's option, competitive civil service status may be granted to a Career Intern who satisfactorily completes the internship and meets all other requirements prescribed by the OPM.

Federal Wage System The pay system used by the Federal Government for positions in blue-collar (crafts, trades, and unskilled labor) occupations. It has multiple pay plans, all starting with W, to distinguish among kinds of work (e.g., WG for Wage Grade nonsupervisory employees, WL for work leaders, and WS for Wage Supervisors). Pay is determined locally through wage surveys.

G

General Schedule (GS) The pay system for white-collar positions in the Federal Government. It has 15 grades (levels of responsibility) with 10 steps (pay rates) per grade.

Generic Rating Procedure A procedure for rating applicants that can be applied to a variety of positions, because the positions have the same general competency/KSA requirements, with the primary difference reflected in the technical specialty areas. Typically, generic rating procedures are most applicable to entry-level positions.

I

Indicator of Proficiency A source of evidence that a candidate possesses job-related competencies/KSAs (e.g., agency certification program, education, experience, professional activity, professional certification).

Interagency Career Transition Assistance Program (ICTAP) This is a process by which Federal employees who have been involuntarily separated may receive selection priority for jobs in agencies other than the one in which they were previously employed.

Interdisciplinary Position A position involving duties and responsibilities closely related to more than one professional occupation. As a result, the position could be classified into two or more professional occupational series. The nature of the work is such that persons with education and experience in two or more professions may be considered equally well qualified to do the work.

J

Job Analysis A systematic method for gathering, documenting, and analyzing information about the content, context, and requirements of the job. It demonstrates that there is a clear relationship between the tasks performed on the job and the competencies/KSAs required to perform the tasks. Job analysis information is used to develop employee selection procedures, identify training needs, define performance standards, and other purposes.

Job Announcement A document that informs the public regarding a job vacancy. A job announcement describes the requirements of the job, and instructs applicants regarding how to apply for the vacancy. Job announcements must be posted on USAJOBS as a means of satisfying the public notice requirement.

Job-Relatedness A standard met when the competencies/KSAs in the rating procedure are shown through an analysis of the job to be necessary for successful job performance.

K

Knowledge (as in Knowledge, Skills and Abilities - KSAs) A body of information applied directly to the performance of a function.

KSAs An acronym for "Knowledge, Skills, and Abilities." An applicant's qualifications for a position are often determined with reference to the KSAs that are relevant to successful performance in that position. Also known as Rating Factors, Selective Placement Factors, Examples, or Quality Ranking Factors.

L

Luevano Consent Decree A court decree entered on November 19, 1981 by the United States District Court for the District of Columbia in the civil action known as Luevano v. OPM and numbered as No. 79-271. The decree became effective on January 18, 1982. The decree has as its purpose the elimination of adverse impact, if any, in the appointment of African Americans and Hispanics to a variety of positions at GS-05 and GS-07 formerly covered by the Professional and Administrative Career Examination (PACE).

M

Merit Promotion Procedures A placement made under the authority of 5 CFR Part 335, "Promotion and Internal Placement." With certain important exceptions (e.g., VEOA) only career status employees may apply for positions that are to be filled under merit promotion procedures.

Minimum Qualifications Qualifications that an applicant must possess, at a minimum, to be eligible to be hired or promoted under the competitive system. Minimum qualifications are typically expressed in terms of job-related years of experience or education (e.g., course credit hours) or a combination of the two. Applicants who do not meet the minimum qualification requirements for the position receive no further consideration.

Multiple Certification The concurrent referral of an applicant to more than one grade, specialty, and/or geographic location. Also known as "dual certification."

N

Non-competitive Action An appointment to or placement in a position in the competitive service that is not made by selection from an open competitive examination, and that is usually based on current or prior Federal service. Noncompetitive actions include (1) all inservice placement actions; (2) appointments of non-Federal employees whose public or private enterprise positions are brought into the competitive service under specific conditions; and (3) appointments and conversions to career and career-conditional employment made under special authorities.

Notice of Results A letter or form that notifies an applicant of the status of his or her application.

O

Objection An agency's request to remove an eligible from consideration on a particular certificate.

Open Period The period during which applications may be submitted for consideration. The duration of the open period must be sufficient to provide adequate public notice of the vacancy, and must be clearly specified in the job announcement. OPM recommends that agencies prescribe an open period of no fewer than five (5) calendar days.

Outstanding Scholar A hiring program created by the Luevano Consent Decree. This program permits the hiring of any individual with a Baccalaureate degree who has at least a 3.5 grade point average on a 4.0 scale or is in the top 10 percent of his or her graduating class (or of a major subdivision, such as a College of Arts and Sciences). The program applies only to entry-level (GS-05 and 07) hiring for specific occupations.

P

Passover Request An objection filed against a preference eligible that, if sustained, would result in the selection of a non-preference eligible.

PATCO An acronym for a system used by the Federal Government to categorize white-collar positions. It stands for Professional, Administrative, Technical, Clerical, and Other.

Pay Banding An alternative approach to Federal white-collar pay where the traditional 15-grade GS system is replaced by pay bands encompassing the minimum and maximum pay rates of 2 or more of the 15 grades. This system gives managers more control over individual movement of employees within the pay bands, and is an essential ingredient to movement toward pay-for-performance in Federal agencies.

Preference Eligible A veteran, spouse, widow, or mother, who meets the definition provided in 5 U.S.C. §2108. Preference eligibles are entitled to have 5 or 10 points added to their earned passing scores on civil service examinations. Preference does not apply, however, to in-service placement actions such as promotions.

Pre-rated Competitor Inventory A list of eligibles that have been rated and ranked and placed in the order in which they are certified, by option and grade. This type of listing has traditionally been called a register, and applications are often referred to as being "pre-rated" or "front-end-rated."

Presidential Management Fellows (PMF) Program Formerly the Presidential Management Intern (PMI) Program, this is a highly competitive hiring program. Its aim is to attract to Federal service outstanding men and women from a variety of academic disciplines and career paths who have a clear interest in, and commitment to, excellence in the leadership and management of public policies and programs. The program is open only to students completing master's or higher level degree programs, and the competitive application process begins at the participating colleges and universities. Presidential Management Fellows receive excepted service appointments at GS-9, may be promoted to GS-11 after 1 year, and at the end of their 2-year fellowship may (at the agency's discretion) noncompetitively be converted to career-conditional or career appointments.

Professional Activity A professional activity is evidence of substantial contributions to a profession that is related to the competencies/KSAs needed to perform the job.

Professional Certification A professional certification is an indicator of proficiency that takes into account a certification that is issued and recognized by a specific general professional community or industry that demonstrates a person's proficiency in the competencies/KSAs needed to perform the job.

Public Notice The process of disseminating job vacancy information in a manner that assures that persons seeking Federal employment will have opportunity to apply for vacancies. Public notice explains to job seekers when, where and how to apply for a Federal job. Public notice is required whenever an agency is considering hiring candidates from outside the Federal workforce for competitive service positions.

Q

Quality Categories Groupings of individuals with similar levels of job-related knowledge, skills, abilities, or competencies.

Quality Level Rating Procedure A rating procedure in which candidates are assigned ratings on qualifying experience and training according to a single quality level. Typically, three quality levels are used: "exceptional," "good," and "minimally qualified."

Quality Ranking Factor Quality ranking factors are competencies/KSAs that are expected to enhance performance in a position. Unlike selective factors, quality ranking factors are not used as a "screen out" factor.

QuickHire The name of a commercial company and of the trademarked automated hiring process that it has developed and that is used by a number of Federal agencies. This automated system receives, tracks, and rates applications.

R

Rating Procedure A single, comprehensive, documented process with specific criteria for making consistent and job-related determinations about the relative qualifications of applicants for a position.

Rating Schedule See "Crediting Plan."

Reemployment Priority List (RPL) A list of employees within the local commuting area who have been separated from an agency because of reduction in force (RIF) or work-related injury. If an employee on the RPL is qualified for a vacancy that exists within his or her local commuting area, an agency must (with few exceptions) select that employee before hiring anyone from outside the agency.

Reinstatement Non-competitive appointment of a person formerly employed in the competitive service (i.e., someone who either had competitive status or was serving probation when separated) into the competitive service as a career or career-conditional employee.

Reinstatement Eligibility The conditions under which a person may be reinstated into the competitive service.

RESUMIX The name of a commercial company and of the trademarked automated hiring process that it has developed and that is used by a number of Federal agencies. This automated system receives, tracks, and rates applications.

Rule of Three A law that requires a selecting official, when selecting from a certificate of eligibles, to make a selection (based solely on merit and fitness) from among the highest three eligibles available for appointment on the certificate.

S

Schedule A Appointment A category of excepted service appointment that applies to positions not of a confidential or policy-determining character, and not in the Senior Executive Service, but for which it is impracticable to apply competitive examining requirements (e.g., qualification standards). Attorneys and chaplains are examples of Schedule A positions.

Schedule B Appointment A category of excepted service appointment that applies to positions not of a confidential or policy-determining character, and not in the Senior Executive Service, but for which it is impracticable to hold open competition or to apply the usual competitive examining procedures. Candidates appointed under Schedule B authority must meet basic qualification requirements established by OPM for the occupation and grade level.

Schedule C Appointment A category of excepted service appointment that applies to positions of a confidential or policy-determining nature.

Selectee A person selected for appointment to a position.

Selecting Official See "Appointing Officer."

Selective Factor A KSA, competency, or special qualification without which a candidate could not perform the duties of a position in a satisfactory manner. Selective factors are applied in addition to minimum qualifications. Applicants who do not meet a selective factor are ineligible for further consideration.

Senior Executive Service (SES) The employment system that applies to positions that are classified above GS-15 and involve executive management and high policy-making responsibilities. SES positions are excluded from the competitive service, the system of rules and regulations that applies to most civil service positions.

Severe Shortage of Candidates A condition where, for a particular position or group of positions, an agency is unable to identify candidates possessing the competencies required to perform the job requirements despite extensive recruitment, extended announcement periods, and the use, as applicable, of hiring flexibilities such as recruitment and relocation incentives.

Skill (as in Knowledge, Skills and Abilities - KSAs) An observable competence to perform a learned psychomotor act.

Standing Inventory An inventory of eligible competitors assigned numerical ratings and certified in score order by occupation, grade, location, etc. Standing inventories are often used when many recurring vacancies are anticipated over time.

Status Applicant An applicant who has satisfied requirements for competitive status.

Status Employee A current Federal employee who has competitive status.

Structured Interview An assessment method in which candidate's job-related competencies/KSAs are evaluated using standard questions that are scored systematically using predetermined criteria or benchmarks. The benchmarks provide behaviorally-specific examples of what constitutes high, medium, and low levels of proficiency. In structured interviews, each candidate is asked the same questions in the same sequence, and their responses are scored according to the predetermined criteria or benchmarks.

Subject-Matter Expert (SME) A person with expert knowledge about what it takes to do a particular job. First-level supervisors are normally good SMEs. Superior incumbents in the same or very similar positions and other individuals can also be used as SMEs if they have current and thorough knowledge of the job's requirements.

Surplus Employee A current agency employee serving under an appointment in the competitive service, and meeting certain other conditions, who has been officially notified that the occupied position is surplus.

T

Temporary Appointment A nonstatus appointment to a competitive service position for a specific time period not to exceed one year.

Term Appointment A nonstatus appointment to a position in the competitive service for a specific period of more than one year and lasting not more than four years.

Test An assessment of a candidate's job-related competencies/KSAs using a series of questions (e.g., true-false, fill-in-the-blank, matching, and multiple choice) or exercises that are administered in a paper-and-pencil or computer format.

Top-of-the-Register See "Rule of Three."

Transmutation Table A mathematical table that is used to convert raw scores obtained by qualified applicants to ratings between 70 and 100.

U

USAJobs A website that provides the public with comprehensive information regarding federal employment. Agencies must post their job vacancy announcements on USAJobs as part of the public notice requirement.

USA Staffing An automated examining system that was developed by OPM and is available to agencies on a reimbursable basis.

V

Vacancy Announcement See Job Announcement.

Validity The degree to which an assessment tool measures the competencies/KSAs important for job performance; i.e., people who score higher on the assessment will do better on the job.

Veterans' Preference A special privilege that entitles qualifying veterans to certain advantages when pursuing Federal employment.

W

Wage Grade See Federal Wage System.

Well-qualified Employee Under CTAP and ICTAP, an eligible employee whose competencies/KSAs clearly exceed the minimum qualification requirements of a vacant position.

Work Sample Assessment An assessment method where a candidate's job-related competencies/KSAs are evaluated through work-specific activity or simulation of a work activity. A writing sample is an example of a work sample assessment.

Federal Job Search Services For Students
www.tenstepsforstudents.org

Federal Resume Critique
Federal resume writing experts will review your federal resume, assessing the following:

- Writing style, content, (including keywords and skills, use of the announcement language, and accomplishments review), federal compliance details, and if the resume is written at the right grade level.
- You will receive a "track changes" critique of your resume with comments for improvement!

$75 critique for students in undergraduate and graduate school.

ONE-ON-ONE CONSULTATION FOR FEDERAL JOB SEARCH STRATEGIES

Speak to a Federal Job Search Consultant concerning your Federal job or internship campaign. Learn to find announcements that you are qualified for and match your resume and skills to these target jobs. A personalized review of your situation saves time and effort in your campaign by targeting the right agencies and jobs! Resume Place Federal Job Search experts consult by telephone/web conference. $100 for 50-minute consultation.

PROJECT ESTIMATE/ASSESSMENT GUIDE FOR FULL-SERVICE WRITING

If you know you are interested in professional writing and editing services for a better Federal resume, Resumix, or KSAs, complete our Student Assessment Guide and submit your resume and announcement for review. We will prepare an estimate for professional services and a strategy to write the best possible application. This is an excellent investment in your Federal career. $45 for Project Estimate / Assessment.

Career Counselors and Teachers Resources
www.tenstepsforstudents.org

Teacher's Section - FREE FOR TEACHERS / COUNSELORS

Student Federal Careers Curriculum PowerPoint Slides CD-ROM
Attention trainers and teachers - FREE if you require the **Student's Federal Career Guidebook** as a required text for your course! Slides take students through each step of the way to a new Federal job or internship. See more information at the website.

Student Federal Careers Teacher's 60-minute Audio
by Authors Kathryn Troutman and Emily Troutman
Free with the use of Real Audio or other audio software
The authors follow the *Ten Steps to Top Jobs and Internships in Government* and the PowerPoint slides to introduce the Ten Steps to a Federal Job program. The two-CD set will serve as an orientation for teachers and students for Federal job search.

Student Federal Careers Curriculum - Free downloadable curriculum
Students can find the federal hiring system convoluted and confusing. The system's complexity makes support invaluable. College instructors and career center trainers can use ideas from The Student's Federal Career Guide to create 6- or 12-week courses. Suggested course outlines for half or full semesters are available at **www.tenstepsforstudents.org**.

For Teachers and Counselors - Get Certified
Certified Federal Job Search Training (CFJST) Program
In today's employment climate, students and alumni need the guidance of qualified professionals more than ever. The comprehensive, easy-to-understand **Federal Job Search Trainer's Certification Program** will ensure that you can effectively guide jobseekers through the government hiring maze. In-depth 3-day program at Loyola College, Columbia, Maryland taught by the author and publisher of this book and 8 other books on Federal Job Search. Information at **www.tenstepsforstudents.org** and**www.resume-place.com**.

About the Authors

Kathryn Kraemer Troutman
For more than 30 years, federal job search and federal resume-writing expert Kathryn Kraemer Troutman has assisted jobseekers with landing jobs with the US government, our nation's largest employer. Her expertise in this marketplace led to Troutman being nicknamed the Federal Job Search Guru. Troutman was also a pioneer in developing and streamlining the format now accepted by government agencies.

Kathryn started The Resume Place, Inc. writing and typesetting resumes for law students from Washington, DC universities. As the Monster.com's Federal Career Coach for the Public Service/ Government Board, many of her questions are from college graduates who are struggling to find career opportunities and who are having trouble figuring out the job titles that are correct for their major.

In 2003, Troutman's book **Ten Steps to a Federal Job** was recognized as the Best Career Book at the Publishers Marketing Association Awards. Her best-selling title, the **Federal Resume Guidebook**, is now out in an all-new 3rd edition, and she has also created a companion CD-ROM of federal resume templates/samples.

Kathryn writes and publishes books on Federal Job Search for current federal employees, mid-career/first-time applicants and now students who are seeking their First Federal Job.

Write to Kathryn at **Kathryn@resume-place.com**

Emily K. Troutman

Emily Troutman graduated from the College of the
Atlantic in Bar Harbor, Maine in 2002 with a Bachelor
of Arts Degree in Human Ecology, and she has since
directed her career toward writing, publishing, public
policy and international affairs in the Middle East. Emily
will complete her Master of Public Policy in May 2005
from the Hubert H. Humphrey Institute, University
of Minnesota.

It was Emily who conceptualized this book's "Find Your
Federal Job" chart, which combines college majors with
desirable federal job titles. Emily began as a editorial consultant for the book,
reading early chapters and offering changes in order to keep the text relevant
for students. Impressed with these ideas, Kathryn realized that her daughter
should be co-author, especially since Emily was in the midst of what became
a successful search for a federal career internship.

Write to Emily at **Emily@resume-place.com**

Emily and Kathryn are available to travel throughout the U.S. to speak at
universities, conferences and radio to help students successfully begin federal
careers.

1 2 3 4 5 6 7 8 9 10

Quasi-official agencies, 45
Question-driven systems, 149-150
QuickHire, 77-78, 185
    example resume, 149-150
    job application process, 149-150
    resume field, 116

R

Raikow, David F., 163
Rating procedure, 186
Rating schedule. See Crediting plan
Recreation: federal jobs, 20
Reemployment Priority List (RPL), 186
Regional Planning: federal jobs, 21
Rehabilitation Science: federal jobs, 20
Reinstatement, 186
Reinstatement eligibility, 186
Relevant courses and descriptions, 110
Research, 106
Research and Engineering Apprenticeship Program (REAP), 27
Research Aquatic Biologist, GS-0401-11, 163
Researchers, 15
Resume Builder electronic resumes, 115
    example, 117-118
Resume Builder Profile, 99-102
Resumes. *See also Federal resumes*
    electronic, 62-63, 97-120
    Federal, 97-123
    formats for student Federal applicants, 117-118, 119-120, 121-122
    what to include, 98
Resumix™, 79, 80-81, 81-82, 83, 84, 115, 186
    example resumes, 117-118
    job application process, 150
Retail Merchandising: federal jobs, 20
Revellier, Marie, 11
Rhetoric: federal jobs, 20
Risk Management: federal jobs, 20
Ritter, Beth Ann, 28
Rule of three, 186
Russian: federal jobs, 20